COSTA RICA

A Guide to the People, Politics and Culture

Tjabel Daling

LATIN AMERICA BUREAU

INTERLINK BOOKS
NEW YORK

This edition first published in 2002

In the U.S.:

Interlink Books
An imprint of Interlink Publishing Group, Inc.
99 Seventh Avenue, Brooklyn, New York 11215 and
46 Crosby Street, Northampton, Massachusetts 01060
www.interlinkbooks.com

Library of Congress Cataloging-in-Publication Data

Daling, Tjabel
Costa Rica in focus: a guide to the people, politics and culture /by Tjabel Daling
p. cm. (In focus)
Includes bibliographical references and index.
ISBN 1-56656-397-6 (pbk)
1. Costa Rica - Guidebooks. 2. Costa Rica - Description and travel I. Title II. Series: In focus (New York, N.Y.)
1998

CIP

In the U.K.:

Latin America Bureau (Research and Action) Ltd,
1 Amwell Street, London EC1R 1UL

The Latin America Bureau is an independent research and publishing organization. It works to broaden public understanding of issues of human rights and social and economic justice in Latin America and the Caribbean.

A CIP catalogue record for this book is available from the British Library
ISBN: 1 899365 16 8

Translation: John Smith
Editing: James Ferguson
Cover photograph: Jevan Berrange/South American Pictures
Cover design: Andy Dark
Design: Liz Morrell
Cartography and diagrams: Kees Prins and Marius Rieff

Already published in the *In Focus* series:
Argentina, Belize, Bolivia, Brazil, Chile, Colombia, Cuba, Dominican Republic, Eastern Caribbean, Ecuador, Guatemala, Haiti, Jamaica, Mexico, Nicaragua, Peru, Venezuela

Printed and bound in Korea

CONTENTS

INTRODUCTION
THE SWITZERLAND OF CENTRAL AMERICA

For half a century Costa Rica has been a byword for democracy and, by the standards of the turbulent Central American region, an oasis of political stability. While in neighboring countries life was until recently dominated by death squads, guerrilla movements, and military dictators, Costa Rica enjoyed political freedoms unknown to El Salvador or Guatemala. With very few exceptions, the last hundred years have seen scarcely any violent conflict. By 1889 the first more or less democratic elections were already being held, beginning a tradition of multi-party elections more akin to Western Europe than Latin America. In contrast with other countries in the region, corruption in Costa Rica is relatively uncommon; a political career is not, as elsewhere, automatically synonymous with self-enrichment and nepotism.

Thanks to "Don Pepe" Figueres, the founder of modern Costa Rica, the country has had no army since 1948, following a brief but bloody civil war. The resources made available by scrapping the military budget were invested by successive reforming Costa Rican governments in education and health care. There has been no political repression since 1948 and human rights are generally respected.

Towards the end of the twentieth century Costa Rica is still a relatively peaceful and stable country. Compared to the inhabitants of most neighboring countries, *Ticos,* as Costa Ricans call themselves, enjoy a reasonable level of prosperity. With its large middle class and tradition of state provision, the country likes to think of itself, albeit with some exaggeration, as the Switzerland of Central America.

All this does not mean, of course, that the country is a trouble-free utopia, and the myth of democratic, prosperous Costa Rica deserves to be examined critically. A quarter of the country's three million people live in poverty and the distribution of wealth is extremely uneven; political power, meanwhile, rests with a small elite. Since the 1970s the country's relative prosperity has been financed in part by state borrowing, and in the 1980s this led to the beginning of an enormous and debilitating debt crisis. The economic pains and austerity measures which have come in the wake of this crisis are creating damaging social tensions, for which Costa Rica's political parties have so far found no solution other than further cuts.

Costa Rica also faces a range of problems due to its geographical position in a region of constant turmoil. The international drug trade has for many years recognized the country's usefulness as a transshipment point for narcotics bound for the USA; the country was pulled into the U.S. contra

Street trading in the center of San José at carnival time *Fotobureau KIT*

war against Nicaragua; while the huge divide in living standards between Nicaragua and Costa Rica has brought about a mass influx of illegal Nicaraguan immigrants.

The advent of eco-tourism, Costa Rica's growth industry, has changed the country's economic profile, bringing difficulties as well as benefits. The steady stream of tourists who descend on Costa Rica's unrivaled natural beauty represent a welcome source of foreign exchange and employment. Yet during the last ten years, tourism has expanded to an extent where the industry is sometimes at odds with environmental protection. Like other eco-tourist destinations, Costa Rica is having to question the long-term value of "green" tourism.

This book looks at Costa Rica's enviable tradition of political stability, while also exploring some of its current predicaments. It traces the evolution of its distinct political culture and examines the economic strains which have threatened its social cohesion. Judging the country's claim to be a leader in environmental planning, it asks whether the Costa Rican model of development is ultimately sustainable under a range of growing pressures.

1 HISTORY AND POLITICS: A COUNTRY DISARMED

Indians and Spaniards

At the beginning of the sixteenth century various groups of Indian peoples were living in what is now Costa Rica, the most developed and important of whom were the Chorotegas. To avoid enslavement by their enemies, their ancestors had fled from Mexico and Guatemala in the eighth century to the Nicoya peninsula and Guanacaste on the Pacific coast.

According to the sixteenth-century Spanish explorer and historian Gonzalo Fernando de Oviedo, the Chorotegas (meaning literally "the people who escaped") were culturally related to the Aztecs and the Mayas and excelled as potters and farmers. They introduced cotton, beans, and cocoa to Costa Rica and traded a range of products, including honey and cotton. The land was under communal ownership and the harvest was distributed according to need. Oviedo also reported that they placated their gods by hurling slaves and virgins at prescribed times into the craters of the country's volcanoes. Some 250 Chorotegas are still living today in the Matambú reserve on the Nicoya peninsula.

Along the Caribbean coast and in the mountainous region where Costa Rica's capital, San José, is now situated, lived the Huetares and their close relatives, the Guatusos, Votos, and Talamancas. It is thought that these indigenous peoples originated from the Caribbean islands and the Amazon region. A third people, the Bruncas, had migrated northwards through the isthmus from modern-day Colombia and Ecuador. They lived from agriculture, hunting, and fishing in the southeastern part of the country. Their metal and gold artifacts can still be admired in many museums throughout the world.

Around 1500 an estimated total of 27,000 people lived in Costa Rica, which was much less densely populated than other areas in the Central American isthmus. The three groups of indigenous peoples frequently waged war against each other. There were other tribes, but very little is known of them.

Columbus and Spanish Colonization

On his fourth journey to the New World, Christopher Columbus landed on September 18, 1502 in the vicinity of modern-day Puerto Limón and was warmly welcomed by the Indians. During his seventeen-day stay Columbus discovered that some of the Indians were wearing articles made of gold, from which the Spaniards assumed that much more gold was to be found further inland, and they accordingly, and optimistically, named the region Costa Rica, meaning "rich coast."

From 1506 the Spaniards tried to colonize the region from Panama but they met with fierce resistance from its indigenous inhabitants. Many colonists died of tropical diseases, lack of food, and from attacks by the Indians. At the same time, many Indians were also dying as a result of diseases such as smallpox and influenza which the Spaniards introduced to the new continent.

In 1524 the first Spanish settlement, "Villa de Bruselas," was established on the Gulf of Nicoya, but after only a few years the colonists had to abandon it, starvation, disease, and attacks from the Chorotegas forcing them into retreat. Some time later, the Spanish virtually wiped out the Chorotegas and sold most of the survivors into slavery in Panama.

It was not until 1563 that Governor Juan Vásquez de Coronado established the first permanent settlement in the Central Plateau: Cartago. The climate there is temperate and much healthier than on the humid Pacific coast, yet for a long time the township remained a very small settlement, and in 1723, when a large part of the town was destroyed by an eruption of the Irazú volcano, there were only some 70 houses there. In 1719, it was recorded that the capital had no barber, doctor, or pharmacist. This backwater remained officially the main town until 1823, when San José became the capital. Earthquakes in 1841 and 1910 further reduced its importance and prosperity.

Colonial Backwater

As part of the Spanish empire, Costa Rica was administered from Guatemala City, where the Captaincy General of Guatemala, a province of the Vice-Kingdom of New Spain (Mexico), was based. For a long time the area was the poorest and most isolated part of Spain's imperial territory. Unlike in Mexico, there were no precious minerals and no mining industry. The Indian population had been almost annihilated as a result of disease and war, and there was no money to buy slaves. As a result, Guatemala's colonial administrators largely left Costa Rica in peace, and there was hardly any communication with the capital, the coasts, or the most important trade routes in the region. These were determining factors for the future of Costa Rica. Large-scale land ownership, which was the norm elsewhere in Central America, only developed to any real extent around Matina, not far from the Caribbean coast, where a number of cocoa plantations were set up to provide the colony's sole export product. The availability of land and the absence of large landowners meant that Costa Rica was spared the sharp inequalities which characterized other Spanish colonial societies.

Some historians maintain that these factors formed the basis for a particular type of rural egalitarianism, for "a nation of equals." Instead of huge estates, small family farms came into being, and the colonists, mostly originating from the Spanish regions of Andalusia and Extremadura, worked their land themselves. In general they were poor and lived isolated lives; a lack of roads ensured that the colonists hardly ever left their own smallholding or village. Not until the eighteenth century did the colony expand and new settlements were established in the central high valley, the *Meseta Central*: Heredia (1706), San José (1737), and Alajuela (1782). The port of Puntarenas on the Gulf of Nicoya was completed about 1800.

The Coffee Aristocracy

Having lost a ten-year fight to keep Mexico, on September 15, 1821 Spain declared its colonies in Central America to be independent; it took a month for the news to reach Costa Rica. Augustín de Iturbide, a former Spanish loyalist general who had crowned himself Emperor of Mexico in 1822, leapt into the power vacuum and proclaimed his rule over all of Central America. The conservative and aristocratic leaders of Cartago and Heredia threw in their lot with the Mexicans, whereas the republicans and liberals of San José and Alajuela were in favor of independence or wanted to form a federal union with the remaining countries of Central America. The result was a short civil war which ended in the liberals' favor. San José became the new capital in 1823, but the decision provoked further resentment and conflict between the four cities.

In 1824 Costa Rica joined the Republic of the United States of Central America (Guatemala, Nicaragua, Honduras, El Salvador, and Costa Rica). This federation was a loose cooperative association, and in the very same year the Costa Ricans elected their own head of state. Juan Mora Fernández, the first president, built houses and schools and distributed free state land to anybody wishing to grow coffee, introduced to Costa Rica from Cuba in 1796. At that time, nearly all state land was unexploited; at independence only 250 square miles of Costa Rica's territory were estimated to be under cultivation.

The Coffee Boom

Coffee was exported for the first time during the administration of Mora Fernández. The beans were mostly produced by small farmers, who sold their crops to the richer farmers, including the few plantation owners, who in turn took over the processing, distribution, and export networks. The larger farmers and merchants profited most from coffee, but small farmers were nonetheless able to maintain their economic independence and avoid working as waged labor on coffee plantations, as was the practice in neighboring countries.

Coffee was instrumental in opening up the world for Costa Rica and made a significant contribution to the democratization of agriculture, at least initially, as the American *Time* journalist William Krehm wrote in his book *Democracies and Tyrannies of the Caribbean*. In the course of the nineteenth century, he observed, coffee was transformed from a mere crop into a national religion.

The government of Braulio Carrillo Colina (1835-1842) continued the policies of Mora Fernández, giving even greater impetus to coffee production and also handing out further expanses of state land to small farmers for coffee growing. Yet Carrillo was no philanthropist, and peasants who failed to cultivate their plots satisfactorily were liable to be flogged. Under Carrillo's autocratic and eccentric rule the Central American Federation collapsed once and for all in 1838, and in 1841 he proclaimed himself dictator for life.

Almost all Costa Rica's coffee was sold to Britain, and British money and manufactures poured into the country. The influx of export earnings and the ever-increasing scale of production created a coffee elite *(la aristocracia cafetalera)*, which became more and more powerful, controlling the national economy and winning overwhelming influence in politics. As Richard Biesanz writes in *The Costa Ricans*, for more than a hundred years the big coffee growers and exporters were the leaders, and in some respects, the owners of the country.

Coffee and Snobbery

"It was the tea-drinking British who were to gild the future of Costa Rican coffee. Right up to 1886, when the Costa Rican railway to the Atlantic was completed, [Captain William] Le Lacheur's sailing vessels made their 140-day voyages from Puntarenas to London via Cape Horn. Costa Rican coffee caught on in England, and the conservatism of the British did the rest. Until the recent war, upper-class families insisted on their Costa Rican coffee because their grandfathers had done so before them. It was largely a private trade to old customers who for flavor and tradition's sake were willing to pay more than world prices. In return Britain became the source of Costa Rica's industrial goods and capital.

Money poured forth from the expanding coffee farms. Clodhoppers wrapped in rags and leaves gave way to opulent planters abreast of Europe's latest fashions. Italian opera companies began arriving. The National Theater of San José, built in the nineties in vague imitation of l'Opéra of Paris, is a monument to the epoch: overnourished angels cavort in stone and paints amidst ornate gold-leafed columns. Italian artists were imported to do the murals. Given this background, coffee in Costa Rica became a religion rather than a mere crop. It was identified with the good things in life, while the foodstuffs were associated with the period of bumpkin backwardness. Whether it paid or not, coffee was grown out of snobbery."

William Krehm, *Democracies and Tyrannies of the Caribbean*, 1984

Monoculture

In order to satisfy increasing demand for the commodity (coffee was becoming a fashionable drink throughout Europe, even in tea-drinking Britain) the small farmers had to introduce technical innovations. These innovations often required considerable investment and many farmers were unable to keep pace with bigger, more modernized producers and were forced to sell their land. Social differences, more or less non-existent in the colonial period, now began slowly to become more marked. The coffee boom had a dramatic economic and social impact, leading to development of the infrastructure and the modernization of the harbor towns of Puerto Limón and Puntarenas. Schools and hospitals were built on the proceeds of coffee exports.

But Costa Rica was developing a monoculture, a dangerous development, which was to have far-reaching negative consequences well into the twentieth century as the country became entirely dependent upon revenue from a single agricultural export. The only other significant export product, introduced at a later stage, was bananas. This monoculture made the national economy extremely vulnerable to over-production and other uncontrollable market developments.

A further drawback of the monoculture syndrome was that Costa Rica began to import a wide range of agricultural products which it could equally well have grown itself. In 1943 the country was importing cereals, sugar, rice, beans, and wheat flour on a huge scale, even though Costa Rica enjoys ideal conditions for the cultivation of all such crops. In the first few decades of this century Costa Rica also imported tens of thousands of cattle every year. Krehm stated that the coffee growers preferred food staples to be imported, with low import tariffs, than for them to be grown at home, thereby ensuring a permanent supply of labor for the plantations. A plentiful agricultural labor force, discouraged from subsistence farming, also meant that plantation owners could keep wages low with the threat of unemployment. The banks were in cahoots with the coffee barons, and only with the greatest reluctance did they provide loans for other, smaller farmers.

In 1848 Juan Rafael Mora Porras, a champion of the coffee aristocracy, was elected president (1848-1859). When he put forward the idea of a state bank which would provide credit for small farmers under favorable conditions, he was brought down by a powerful clique of coffee planters. A year later Mora Porras attempted a counter-coup; it failed and he had to face the firing squad.

Richard Biesanz points out that the coffee barons did not always share identical political interests. They were, however, all very close to power or, in some cases, exercised direct political power. Political allies and enemies were very often members of the same family. Members of the armed forces, who in the notorious and politically unstable 1860s carried out a number of coups and deposed presidents, were either members of the coffee elite or subordinated to it.

National Heroes

It was during the presidency of Mora Porras that the bizarre rise of the American adventurer, William Walker, was brought to a halt. In 1855 Walker had arrived in Nicaragua with 58 supporters, at the invitation of the Liberal Party, which at the time was embroiled in a power struggle with the Conservatives, and the same year he had himself crowned "President of the Republic of Nicaragua." In Nicaragua Walker re-introduced slavery and developed a scheme to turn the whole of Central America into a sort of U.S. colony.

In February 1856 Mora Porras declared war on Walker, but not on Nicaragua. Within weeks he had put together a motley army of 9,000 people, men and women, recruited from among farmers, clerks, and merchants, and armed with machetes, old rifles, and farm implements. In 1857 Walker's troops marched into Guanacaste. Although ravaged by a cholera epidemic, Mora Porras' troops inflicted a crushing defeat on Walker's forces. Walker himself escaped, only to undertake further adventures until his execution in Honduras in 1860.

The story goes that a certain Juan Santamaría, a nineteen-year-old drummer, put Walker to flight by setting fire to his wooden fort, but that he lost his own life in the process. This feat of arms brought Santamaría eternal fame as a Costa Rican patriot. The international airport in San José bears his name and Alajuela, the town where he was born, reveres his memory with a museum and a statue.

On his return home Mora Porras was blamed for the death of thousands of people, principally those who had succumbed to cholera. Almost ten per cent of the then population died in the battle against Walker's megalomania. Nevertheless, Mora Porras was later rehabilitated and despite his execution in 1860 at the hands of his opponents is also regarded as a national hero today.

United Fruit and the Atlantic Railway

The goal of fettering the power of the coffee barons was to some extent achieved by General Tomás Guardia, who came to power in 1870 following a coup and ruled dictatorially until 1882. During his administration, work was begun on laying the railway line from San José to the Caribbean port of Puerto Limón, funded by large loans from a British bank. The decision to build the railway line was made under pressure from the coffee barons, since Costa Rica needed an Atlantic port in order to streamline coffee exports. Shipping the coffee through Puerto Limón meant that the coffee could be on the European markets three months earlier than previously. The Panama Canal was not opened until 1914.

The railway line was built by black workers recruited from the Caribbean, particularly Jamaica, and by Italians and Chinese, taking it through the jungle and high over the mountains. The railway was nineteen years in the making and 4,000 workers lost their lives. Guardia negotiated the project with the American capitalist Henry Meiggs, who had already built railway lines in Chile and Peru. Meiggs' nephew, Minor Cooper Keith, started the work in 1872. When during the course of laying the line the money ran out, Keith hit upon the idea of setting up banana plantations along the track, realizing the export potential of bananas. In 1884 Keith concluded an agreement with President Bernardo Soto whereby he took over the British debt in exchange for large expanses of land along the railway line and the right to use the railway line. He also ensured that he would be exempted from paying tax for twenty years. In 1899 he established the United Fruit Company, which was to wield huge social and political influence in Central America for many years.

The railway line was finally completed in 1890 and was of immense social significance. Until 1970 it was the only connection between the Central Plateau and Puerto Limón and was the principal means of transport for many people who lived in small villages along the railway line. The train to and from Puerto Limón had a life-span of exactly one hundred years; in 1990 an earthquake made it impossible for further trains to use the mountain route and since then trains only run in the Caribbean lowland.

Remarkably, the wealthy coffee oligarchy hardly invested at all in the new, capital-intensive banana industry. Perhaps fearing the rise of a rival agrarian elite, the coffee barons ignored the potential of bananas, leaving the banana-producing regions in the province of Limón as isolated enclaves under the control of North Americans, a situation which remained unchanged for many decades.

Democracy

During Guardia's dictatorship, republican and liberal ideas had gained in influence, and his regime was followed a period of almost 40 years during which liberalization and democratization made noticeable advances. This period was dominated by growing tensions between the conservative Catholic Church and largely liberal governments. Laws were introduced

Transporting bananas on the United Fruit Company's plantations near Limón c.1910 *Fotobureau KIT*

which aimed to separate church and state. Liberal governments secularized cemeteries, evicted the Jesuits and prohibited the establishment of monastic orders. The role of the church in education was severely restricted and the government closed the Catholic University of Santo Tomás, arguing that education should be free and state-administered.

During the same period political parties emerged which did not merely act as vehicles for *caudillos* or local barons, but which developed distinctive policies and ideas. There was freedom of the press. In 1889 the first more or less democratic elections were held, without any interference from the government. Two presidential candidates conducted an orderly and peaceful campaign and even visited the country's remotest villages in search of voters, male and white, of course. Women, blacks, and Indians were not yet allowed to vote.

The Liberals campaigned on the slogan that the people were part of the decision-making process. Ironically, democracy worked so well that a majority of the electorate voted for the opposition, and when supporters of the ruling Liberals threatened not to accept the election victory of opposition candidate José Joaquín Rodriguez, some 10,000 armed members of the opposition took to the streets. The Liberals gave in and recognized the first democratically-elected president, Rodriguez, who, as chance would have it, turned out to be an authoritarian ruler.

The Last Civil War

Even after 1889, opposition leaders were exiled, civil rights were suspended, and coups did still occur, although something resembling democracy was beginning to emerge. That tradition has now lasted for more than a hundred years, albeit with a few exceptions, such as the coup which Federico Tinoco, the Minister for War, carried out in 1917, an event which revealed the continuing power of the coffee aristocracy. The planned introduction of income tax by the then president, Alfredo González Flores, was anathema to the coffee elite and their merchant allies; they gave their support to Tinoco, who stifled press freedoms and imprisoned his political opponents. One-and-a-half years later, Tinoco was deposed, not least thanks to popular protest and the refusal of the United States to recognize his administration.

Modern democracy in Costa Rica took its de facto form in 1948. The election results of that year were declared invalid by an unlikely coalition of Social Conservatives and Communists, under the leadership of Rafael Angel Calderón and Teodoro Picado. The poll had been won by Otilio Ulate, the candidate of the National Unity Party (PUN), a newspaper owner representing the coffee aristocrats who opposed Calderón. Calderón was a conservative, but one with reformist Christian-social ideas, who was supported by the communists of Manuel Mora and the Catholic Church under Archbishop Victor Sanabría. During his presidency (1940-44) he had carried through extensive social reforms, winning both the admiration of the poor and the odium of the old elite.

In 1944 Calderón's puppet-candidate Picado won the elections by dint of fraud (Calderón was constitutionally disqualified from a second consecutive term) and for the first time farmers, businessmen, young intellectuals, and trade unionists turned against him. When, four years later, Congress, controlled by Calderón and Picado, refused to accept Ulate's victory, Calderón's opponents took up arms. The most important figure within this movement was the coffee planter,José María Figueres, a convinced anti-communist. A short, though bloody, civil war broke out.

On April 18, 1948 government troops surrendered, and for eighteen months Figueres led a junta which established a new constitution. In 1949 Figueres handed over power to Ulate, the legitimately elected president. Calderón did in fact make a further, and abortive, attempt to seize power from Nicaragua; in 1958 he returned from exile and in 1962 even took part in elections again, yet despite winning 35 per cent of the vote, he failed to win a second period of office.

Calderón and Figueres in San José's National Museum

Tjabel Daling

The Legacy of Calderón and Figueres

During his administration Calderón introduced the minimum wage, the eight-hour working day, and health insurance. He gave workers trade union rights and authorized legislation allowing free collective bargaining in workplaces; he also introduced land reforms. To everybody's amazement, Figueres, the coffee baron, not only retained these social reforms but even extended them. Figueres, affectionately known as "Don Pepe" as a token of his popularity, twice held the office of president, from 1954 to 1958 and from 1970 to 1974, and in Costa Rica he is still generally viewed as a champion of democracy. His 1949 constitution is still in force, a constitution which abolished the army and gave the vote to women, blacks, and Indians. Banks and insurance companies were nationalized and under the aegis of Figueres' National Liberation Party (PLN) the role of the state in social and economic life increased enormously.

Manuel Mora

Manuel Mora Valverde died in 1994 at the age of 85. He was the last of the four great political leaders of the 1940s, together with Calderón, Archbishop Sanabría, and José María Figueres. Mora was widely respected in Costa Rica, although he never renounced his commitment to communism. Even after the fall of the Berlin Wall, Mora did not believe that communism was bankrupt, asking: "Is poverty defeated? Has social injustice disappeared? Until that happens there will be a reason for socialism."

Mora set up the Communist Party in 1929 at the age of nineteen. A few years later he organized a major strike on banana plantations around Puerto Limón, which the government put down with force. But for many years afterwards, the influence of the communists on the plantation workers held firm.

Because of his alliance with the Social-Conservative President Calderón and the Catholic Church, Mora is regarded as one of the founders of Costa Rica's modern welfare state. He was the commander of the government forces

which in 1948 were mobilized against Figueres' troops. Costa Rican historians maintain that the peace which the two politicians subsequently concluded brought about decades of stability and calm. For Mora, the crucial issue was that Calderón's social reforms should remain in place, and when Figueres assured him that he was seeking to extend those reforms, a peace agreement was reached. In Costa Rican political mythology, Mora has entered history as a man who considered national interests more important than partisan ambition, and President José María Figueres has called him a "patriot and a leader." Mora's most trenchant critics came from the ranks of his own party, especially from its Stalinist wing. They accused him of rejecting revolution as a means of bringing about social change and of opportunism in his alliance with Calderón.

Opinions vary considerably on the legacy of the 1940s. The *Calderonistas* are adamant that they fought for the preservation of social reforms, while the *Figueristas* maintain that they took up arms against corruption and the influence of the communists. Wherever the truth may lie, the 1948 civil war and the 1949 constitution represent in various ways a watershed in the history of Costa Rica. The social reforms have remained in place, and since 1948 no government has come to power through violent means, a situation which is unique in Latin America. In intervening years the reactionary coffee aristocracy has gradually lost influence in favor of the liberal consensus which advocates the extension of the welfare state.

The abolition of the Costa Rican military is perhaps the most remarkable legacy of 1948-9. In removing the army as a political actor, Figueres wanted to break the power of the old elites and the coffee oligarchy in particular. Elite factions, he believed, had too often used the army to put a puppet government in power, and the military had chosen to oppose Figueres in the civil war. In an interview in 1984, Don Pepe even maintained that he had abolished two armies, the defeated government forces and the victorious guerrilla army.

Calderón and Figueres remain well-known names in Costa Rican politics since their sons, Rafael Angel Calderón and José María Figueres Olsen have followed in their fathers' footsteps. The former, the leader of the Christian-Social Unity Party (PUSC), was president between 1990 and 1994 and Figueres was elected in 1994.

The Costa Rican Model

For many years following 1948, political life in Costa Rica was dominated by the PLN, formed by Figueres in 1951 and which had a majority in parliament until 1978, even under Conservative presidents. A Conservative coalition of the National Republican Party (Calderón's supporters) and

Ulate's PUN provided the president in 1958 and 1966, even though during the 1948 revolution the two parties were sworn enemies.

President Mario Enchamdi (1958-1962) was an advocate of free-market economics and he attempted to restrict the role of the state in the economy and to roll back the policies of the previous PLN governments. He was no more successful in this than José Joaquín Trejos Fernández (1966-1970), who failed in the same objective.

The PLN, meanwhile, developed a consensual fusion of socialist, liberal and Christian-social ideas. Espousing social-democratic reformism, the party insisted that the state had a significant role to play within a capitalist economy. Under the direction of the PLN, Costa Rica continued to move in the direction of a welfare state during the 1960s and 1970s, with the emphasis on health, education, and infrastructure. According to successive PLN governments, better education and the expansion of roads and ports were vital preconditions for the modernization of the economy, which still depended first and foremost on coffee and banana exports.

The backbone of the party has traditionally been formed by small farmers, the urban middle class, aspiring entrepreneurs, and intellectuals. Under PLN administrations in the 1960s and 1970s, the apparatus of government increased considerably as the party tried to achieve its goal of full employment by expanding the public-sector payroll. Government employment increased two-fold between 1950 and 1963, bringing problems as well as social benefits. State-sector jobs increasingly became the preserve of *liberacionistas* (PLN supporters), and the bureaucracy swelled accordingly.

The expansion of social provision was vigorously continued in the 1970s by Figueres and his PLN successor Daniel Odúber Quirós, while the Conservative president, Rodrigo Carazo Odio (1978-82) did little to reverse the trend. Yet harsh economic realities were already beginning to threaten the social-democratic model. The fact that the welfare state could only be financed through foreign loans following the oil crisis of 1973 (and even more so after the second crisis in 1979) was at first dismissed by politicians of all parties as "irrelevant" and it was only with the next PLN president, Luis Alberto Monge (1982-1986), that the growing debt crisis was confronted. It is since his administration that the terms "retrenchment" and "privatization" have featured significantly in practically every government memorandum. Since Monge, every Costa Rican president has been forced to grapple with the country's intractable economic difficulties, and the welfare state has often come a poor second to the requirements of structural adjustment imposed by international financial institutions.

Costa Rica and Central America

Monge's predecessor, Carazo, had already had to deal with the second problem facing Costa Rica in the 1980s: the extremely volatile political situation in a number of neighboring countries. Civil wars had raged in Guatemala, El Salvador, and Nicaragua in the 1970s and 1980s, costing the lives of tens of thousands of people. Left-wing (and in Guatemala, Indian) guerrilla fighters fought bitter wars with U.S.-backed national armies to challenge the power of ruling oligarchies. In Guatemala and El Salvador, right-wing death squads and paramilitary groups wiped out whole villages in counter-insurgency campaigns.

Sandinistas and Contras

In Nicaragua the left-wing Sandinistas (FSLN) ousted the dictator Anastasio Somoza in 1979, following a two-year conflict in which 30,000 Nicaraguans died. After the Sandinista victory, war continued on a smaller scale, this time between the FSLN government and the U.S.-sponsored Contras, their right-wing opponents. In the 1980s Costa Rica's other immediate neighbor, Panama, was dominated by the drugs mafia and its military frontman, General Manuel Noriega.

During the last twenty years there have been frequent diplomatic incidents between Costa Rica and Nicaragua. Initially Costa Rica supported the FSLN in its struggle against the Somoza family which had ruled Nicaragua since the 1930s as its personal fiefdom. At the end of the 1970s, during the presidency of Rodrigo Carazo, the northern part of Costa Rica served as a Sandinista base, from which guerrillas launched attacks on Somoza's troops. After the FSLN victory in 1979, however, the enthusiasm of Costa Rican politicians for the Sandinistas cooled somewhat since socialist reforms and reluctance to hold elections ran counter to the Costa Rican conception of democracy. Subsequently, under pressure from the United States, Costa Rica was even forced to allow Nicaraguan Contras to operate freely from Costa Rican territory, leading to a deterioration in relations with the Sandinista government in Managua. From 1983 onwards, large amounts of U.S. aid flowed into Costa Rica, fending off bankruptcy as the country faced its traumatic debt crisis. Policy towards the Sandinistas duly took a more pro-Washington stance.

In order to prevent Costa Rica becoming involved in the war in Nicaragua, the PLN president, Luis Alberto Monge, proclaimed in 1983 a state of "permanent, active, and armed neutrality." He had Contra camps closed and arrested Contra leaders such as the notorious ex-Sandinista "Commandante Cero," Eden Pastora. Nevertheless, Nicaraguan rebels continued to use Costa Rica in subsequent years as a base, while the Sandinista airforce even undertook air sorties over Costa Rican territory.

President Oscar Arias receives 1987 Nobel Peace Prize from ex-president Carlos Andrés Pérez of Venezuela (right) and Willy Brandt (center). *ANP*

Monge's cabinet was divided over policy towards Managua, and in July and August the two countries seemed on the verge of open hostilities.

Arias and the Nobel Peace Prize

Under the PLN president, Oscar Arias Sánchez (1986-1990), Costa Rica's policy of neutrality took on a clearer shape. Arias launched a successful peace plan for Central America, for which in October 1987 he was awarded the Nobel Peace Prize. "A tractor is much more useful than a tank" was one of his slogans.

Arias' peace policy marked an important advance on the failed initiative formulated by Mexico, Venezuela, Colombia, and Panama, known as the Contadora group. Where the Contadora group emphasized in its plan the "national sovereignty of the Central American countries," Arias stressed "internal democratization." The presidents of El Salvador, Nicaragua, Guatemala, Honduras, and Costa Rica signed the peace agreement in the Guatemalan city of Esquipulas in August 1987. It led eventually to democratic elections in Nicaragua, the departure of the Contras from Honduras and Costa Rica, and negotiations between the government and the rebels in El Salvador and Guatemala.

Arias has continued to work for peace. He was instrumental in the abolition of the army in Haiti in 1995, and earlier that year, together with the former U.S. president, Jimmy Carter, he appealed to Peru and Ecuador to cease hostilities when the two countries went to war over a disputed piece of border territory. In June 1995 he visited Cuba in an attempt to mediate between the U.S. and Fidel Castro's government. In April 1997, in the presence of twenty Latin American presidents, Arias suggested a complete moratorium on arms sales in the region and a series of treaties to avoid any future arms race.

A Country Disarmed

In keeping with the country's reputation for pacifism and in the spirit of Arias, Costa Rica proposed in the United Nations that a worldwide cease-fire should be observed for a week in October 1995. The idea was conceived to mark the fiftieth anniversary of the international organization and was also intended to reinforce Costa Rica's image as an active exponent of peace. A Costa Rican columnist wrote, "Only our country has the moral strength to take this initiative." And it was this moral strength which President Figueres invoked when, at the beginning of 1995, he announced that he wished to have Costa Rica's neutrality enshrined in its constitution. During the volatile years of the mid-1980s, when conflict with Nicaragua seemed likely, former presidents Figueres, Odúber, and Carazo issued a joint statement which read: "The dignity of our people does not require violent or aggressive gestures and attitudes but rather sensitivity and the understanding traditional throughout our history."

In Costa Rica pacifism has come to be seen as an almost national characteristic and features in many dimensions of political life. The government, for instance, has prevented a large number of allegedly violent and pornographic films from being shown on television and has banned similar material on video. It claims, and many Costa Ricans agree, that violence is inimical to national culture. Public opinion overwhelmingly rejects violence, political or otherwise, and most Costa Ricans are proud that their country does not have an army. Justifying the censorship of imported films, Enrique Castillo, the minister of justice, has said, "What I sometimes see on the television is pure and gratuitous violence, which can have a very negative impact, a degree of violence that is quite at odds with the individual temperament of most *Ticos*."

2 THE ECONOMY: THE WELFARE STATE UNDER PRESSURE

With a foreign debt of almost $4 billion, Costa Rica faces two other overwhelming economic problems: its balance-of-payments deficit and the government's budget deficit. In simple terms, the country imports more than it exports, while the state spends more money than it raises. Notwithstanding increasing revenue over recent years from tourism and exports, the balance-of-payments deficit in January 1995 was eight per cent higher than in the previous year. In 1996 the budget deficit amounted to five per cent of Gross Domestic Product (GDP), following a record 8.3 per cent deficit in 1995. As usual, the deficit had also risen steeply in the two previous years, years which were dominated by the election campaign and government spending on votes.

Burden of Debt

Following the Mexican debt crisis of 1981, it became clear that Costa Rica was also in very deep financial difficulties. The country had a foreign debt of almost $2.7 billion, almost the highest per capita debt in the world. Nevertheless, President Carazo (1978-82) took no radical measures to address the country's spectacular indebtedness. High coffee prices in 1976 and 1977 had simply given Costa Rica the comforting delusion that there was nothing wrong, and as Alonso Trejos observes, "The people and the government acted as if they could go on spending forever."

The oil crises of 1973 and 1979 should have been warnings that the country was living on borrowed time. Costa Rica has almost no mineral resources and has to import all its oil. The enormous increases in oil prices pushed its balance of trade totally out of equilibrium and meant that government spending could only be maintained at the same level by further loans. A collapse in world coffee prices in 1978 merely worsened the country's economic situation.

Carazo continued to borrow money abroad, but in 1981 was forced unilaterally to suspend interest payments to foreign creditors. Yet he still refused to carry out the large-scale structural adjustment program demanded by the International Monetary Fund (IMF) as its condition for granting balance-of-payment support. When the IMF duly halted credit facilities, Carazo attempted to crank up exports and restrict imports by a drastic devaluation of the colón, but there was little left to rescue. The budget deficit rose in 1982 to sixteen per cent, inflation soared to almost one 100 per cent, and the country's poor bore the brunt of steep price rises and falling living standards. Production collapsed, salaries dropped sharply, and unemployment rose dramatically. In 1981 and 1982 the country experienced an economic recession which shrank GDP by 2.3 and 7.3 per cent respectively.

Carazo's successor, the social-democratic President Monge, restored relations with the IMF in December 1982, and Costa Rica was given a new loan of $92 million. What the country was forced to offer in return was the dismissal of thousands of government employees, a sharp increase in taxes, rises in a number of excise duties (on fuel, imports, electricity), the reduction of the government deficit, drastic cuts in social spending, the postponement of investment programs, and the sale of state-owned companies. From now on Costa Rica's economic fate was largely determined by the IMF and Monge was given the ambiguous and unflattering nickname "Mr. Fondo" (meaning "Mr. Fund" or, alternatively, "Mr. Bottom"). Monge, for his part, insisted that Costa Rica had no option but to embrace structural adjustment after years of high borrowing and spending: "Many feared a few years ago that Costa Rica would fall prey to the same chaos as had the other countries in Central America. Our medicine is, and was, bitter, but we have avoided chaos." Monge realized that a final break with the IMF and the suspension of debt repayments would make Costa Rica a pariah in international financial circles.

Two Costa Ricas

Under Monge and his fellow social-democratic successor, Oscar Arias Sánchez (1986-90), the economy recovered to some extent. Inflation fell to twelve per cent in 1984, the budget deficit gradually decreased and there was modest economic growth for several years. Public-sector pay, however, declined by about a quarter in real terms during the 1980s. Debt rescheduling which followed the IMF agreement gave the Monge administration some breathing space, deferring large interest payments for several years. What also proved to be a lifeline was the financial support of the United States, which gave and lent Costa Rica some $200 million each year between 1983 and 1986, almost a third of the total government deficit. For Washington, Costa Rica was of considerable strategic importance as a buffer against the left-wing Sandinista government in Nicaragua, and the country briefly became the world's largest per capita recipient of U.S. aid after Israel.

In spite of U.S. funding, Costa Rica continued to struggle with chronic balance-of-payments problems. Widespread cuts in government expenditure led to serious social problems. Further debt forgiveness and rescheduling in the shape of the Brady Plan (commercial debts) and the Paris Club (the cartel of rich creditor governments) brought some temporary relief in 1989 and 1990, but by 1993 it had already risen again to over $4 billion.

Arias's PLN government adopted an ambitious macro-economic adjustment policy, aiming to further reduce the role of the state while attempting to offset the impact of such policies with social compensation measures. Subsidies to farmers were slashed, and under IMF pressure consumption taxes were imposed on a wide range of goods. His successor, Rafael Angel Calderón (1990-4) of the Christian-Social Unity Party (PUSC), continued the restructuring process in order to reduce the government's debts and deficits even further.

Under both Arias and Calderón prices rose much more quickly than the minimum wage. To many, the economic programs of the PLN and PUSC were almost indistinguishable in practice, but politicians from both parties tried to suggest otherwise. In 1994 the PLN presidential candidate, José María Figueres, spoke in his election campaign about the "two Costa Ricas" of his predecessor: the Costa Rica of the rich, with their private schools and hospitals, and the other Costa Rica, with overcrowded classrooms, underpaid teachers, an overburdened health care service, and a government which ignored small farmers and the urban poor. He promised that the neo-liberal Costa Rica of Calderón would be replaced by a "social Costa Rica." After a decade of widespread cuts, he pledged, his government would once again begin to invest in new roads, education, and social services.

Figueres, a former minister of agriculture under Arias, initially tried to raise revenue by increasing fuel and electricity prices and deregulating prices for basic foodstuffs. The IMF, World Bank, and Inter-American Development Bank, meanwhile, demanded the sacking of 8,000 state employees over four years as the condition for $350 million of loans. Like his predecessors, Figueres rapidly found himself squeezed between his populist pledge to preserve the welfare state and the neo-liberal policy program of the international lenders.

The Calderón-Figueres Pact

Concern about the high budget deficit, the deficit in the balance of payments, the huge domestic debt which swallowed up half the government's budget, the expensive pension system, and fear that the IMF would impose sanctions forced Figueres to take an unusual step. In the spring of 1995, following secret talks with Calderón, his predecessor from the opposition PUSC, he announced a bipartisan pact on economic policy, hence winning a broad political basis for his radical retrenchment plans. With his own PLN holding a parliamentary majority of only one, Figueres announced that only cross-party agreement would save Costa Rica from a "period of ungovernability and a serious economic crisis."

The agreement marked a dramatic about-turn of traditional PLN state-centered policy. Among a range of neo-liberal reforms, it projected: the raising of sales taxes; the reduction of the budget deficit to one per cent of GDP (a measure to be enshrined in the constitution); reform of the pension system; the merging of ministries; the merging and closing of some state agencies and the privatization of a large number of other state institutions. The last category included, for example, the Industrial and Agricultural League for Sugar-Cane (LAICA), the National Institute for Cooperative Promotion (INFOCOOP), the National Directorate for Community Development (DINADECO), the Coffee Institute (ICAFE), the National Banana Corporation (CORBANA), the Rice Office (OFIARROZ), and the Directorate for Tobacco.

Within the PLN the deal between Figueres and Calderón caused widespread anger, particularly the proposal to reform the banking system, a state monopoly since 1949. "The last dogma falls," claimed the newspaper *La Prensa Libre*. For PLN traditionalists, allied to the trade unions, Figueres' free-market reforms were an almost sacrilegious betrayal of party principle.

Since 1995 Figueres's economic policy has vacillated between renewed plans for privatization and conciliation with the trade unions and PLN activists who oppose such schemes. Relations with the PUSC have gradually soured, while Figueres remains unpopular within his own party. The IMF has also been critical of the government, condemning its inability to close the fiscal deficit and threatening to withdraw further support. Problems worsened after an economic recession in 1996, when the government's internal debt rose to $3.5 million, or around twenty per cent of GDP, a very high figure for a small country like Costa Rica. The value of salaries has also fallen steadily, by five per cent during 1996-7 alone. Figueres insists, however, that Costa Ricans will soon experience the benefits of economic reform; "the last three years," he declared in May 1997, "have been more a time for sowing than reaping."

Figueres is proud of his efforts to reduce interest rates, control inflation, invest in housing, and reform the constitution to guarantee six per cent of the national budget for education. Yet a majority of Costa Ricans remain opposed to his neo-liberal program, while his administration has also been damagingly linked to several serious corruption scandals. In a 1997 public opinion poll, Figueres received a rating of "bad" or "very bad" from 52 per cent of those polled. His unpopularity bodes ill for José Miguel Corrales, the PLN presidential candidate for elections in February 1998, who was lagging behind the PUSC's Miguel Angel Rodríguez in 1997 opinion polls. Since recent elections in Costa Rica have produced almost automatic PLN-PUSC alternations, a change of government looks likely.

The Traditional Economy

Bananas are Costa Rica's single most important export, and the country is the world's second biggest exporter after Ecuador. Exports earned $580 million in 1995, surpassed only by tourism's $661 million. Approximately 50,000 people depend directly or indirectly on the sector which accounts for a fifth of all exports. Three multinational companies, Chiquita Brands (formerly the United Fruit Company), Standard Fruit/Dole, and Del Monte account for virtually the whole distribution and export side of the industry; small independent and national growers produce half or more of the bananas.

The Costa Rican government has tried over the course of time to improve the status of the independent growers relative to the "big three" multinationals, who have been pressured to pay the national producers a better price for their bananas. The government also set up ASBANA, a cooperative enterprise whose task it is to promote the mutual interests of the national producers.

Since 1994 the banana industry has found itself in the doldrums, as growers have been faced with high interest rates, large debts, and low prices on the world market. On some plantations an outbreak of "Black Sigatoka" disease, a poisonous leaf fungus, has caused a 30 per cent drop in production. Companies in the province of Limón, where most of the bananas are cultivated, have also had to contend with drought. In 1996 the Fyffes banana company sold the large plantation it had acquired months earlier, the plantation having made losses of $45 million over three years.

Euro Bananas and Dollar Bananas

A further blow to Costa Rica's banana industry came in the form of the European Union's ruling in July 1993 that banana imports from Latin American countries, including Costa Rica, were to be restricted, giving preference to bananas from former European colonies in the Africa, Caribbean, and Pacific (ACP) grouping. The EU banana regime actively limited so-called "dollar bananas" from Latin America, favoring those from ex-colonies such as Jamaica and the Windward Islands. The agreement was put into effect against the will of Germany, Belgium, and The Netherlands, the EU countries which have traditionally imported bananas on the open market.

Under the terms of the agreement, Latin American countries were obliged to cut their exports from 2.4 million tons in 1993 to 2.1 million in 1994 and 2.2 million in 1995, with exports in excess of 2 million tons attracting a higher rate of duty. Originally the Latin American countries had demanded a quota of 2.5 million tons, but Costa Rica, Colombia and Nicaragua eventually changed their position in 1994, to the indignation of the U.S., accepting a 23 per cent share of the EU market. Ecuador and Guatemala, meanwhile, continued to oppose the agreement.

According to the United States, the EU's banana regime is damaging to American companies and violates international trade laws, and in October 1994 the U.S. government launched an investigation into the EU's "discriminatory practices." According to their own estimates, American companies saw their sales to the EU halved and in 1995 the USA lodged a complaint against the EU with the World Trade Organization (WTO). Under pressure, the EU agreed to raise the "dollar banana" quota to 2.35 million tons in early 1996, but this failed to prevent the WTO from ruling against the EU in 1997. Costa Rica has welcomed the WTO ruling, especially since the powerful "big three," with interests in the country, are liable to benefit from increased access to Europe.

The banana trade war has put relations between the Costa Rica and the U.S. under pressure, since Costa Rica agreed terms with Brussels and abandoned the U.S. campaign to scrap the EU regime. Colombia and Costa Rica, conversely, have pointed out that the U.S. government failed to support them when they opposed the quota regulation. Besides which, San José claims, Washington also maintains quotas, for the import of textiles, beef, and sugar. In November 1996 Costa Rica won a small victory when the WTO ruled that U.S. restrictions on exports of underwear from the country were illegal.

Costa Rica has been able to contain the damage caused by export market restrictions by selling bananas into other markets (the United States and Eastern Europe), although at lower prices. It will also benefit from increased access into the EU market if the banana regime is, as predicted, reformed. However, bad weather and low prices continued to plague the sector in 1996 and 1997.

Working Conditions

Banana production has generally increased as a result of relative employment stability in the industry during recent years. Strikes are no longer a regular occurrence on the smaller-scale nationally owned plantations or those of the big multinational companies. The power of the communist-dominated trade unions, which were once so strong, has disappeared (see Chapter 3) and some aspects of working conditions have improved, although they are still far from ideal.

The government, employers, and trade unions, however, have very different ideas about further improvements in the working and living conditions of the workers. At the end of 1994, the multinational Standard Fruit/Dole opened a model village twenty miles south of the port town of Limón, Bananito Sur. It is a community of 127 houses, a bank, a health care clinic, a park, a school, and other facilities. For government and Standard officials, it is a model of

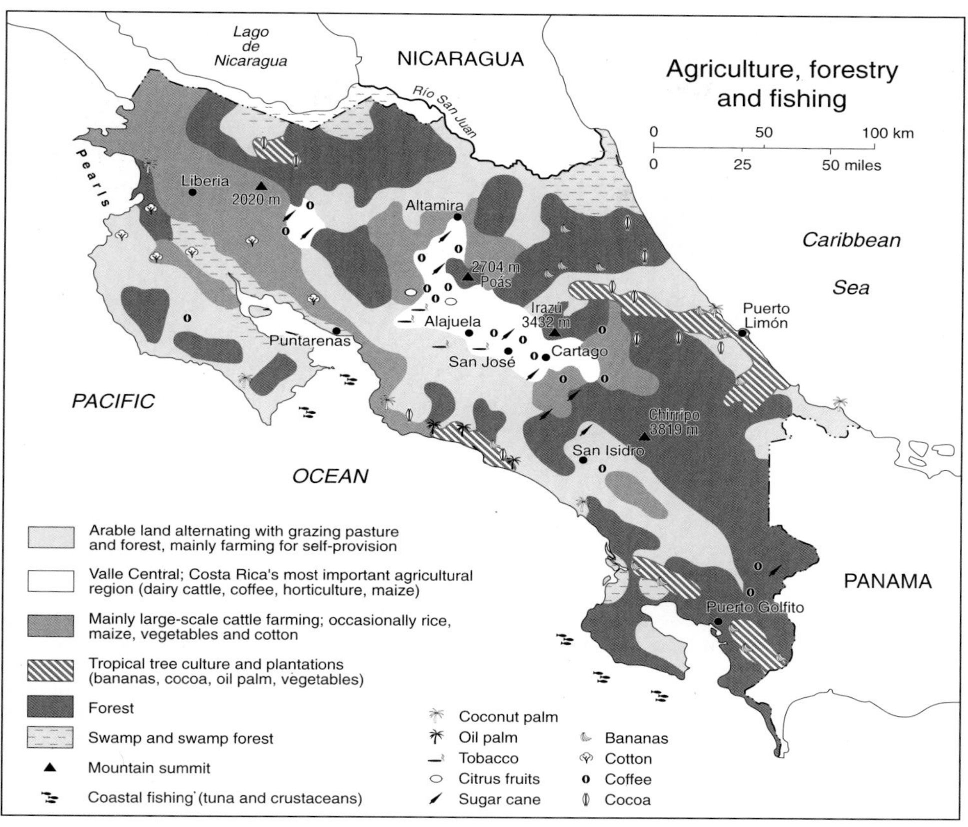

what a "banana town" ought to look like, and Standard prides itself on the fact that its workers are so well-treated that there has been no strike for fifteen years. According to the company, its workers earn an average of $14 a day, well above the minimum wage.

The trade unions in the banana industry take a different view. "Everything being done for the workers is tremendous, but this is a cosmetic village," says trade union leader, Ramón Barrantes. Trade union representatives point out the many infringements of health and safety regulations in banana processing (large quantities of insecticide are handled); they also allege that multinationals actively oppose the setting up of unions, reject collective employment agreements, and offer poor wages, which in the banana sector are among the lowest in the country. There are many banana workers in Costa Rica earning only one dollar an hour, even with Standard/Dole.

Confronted with such conditions, the banana unions, working in collaboration with the Foro Emaus (Emmaus Forum), have drawn up a charter with thirteen minimum working condition norms. These include the right to social security, the right to work in a clean environment, the right to collective bargaining, and the prohibition of child labor. The Emmaus Forum is a collaborative association of environmental organizations, the Catholic Church and human rights organizations.

Coffee

San José's splendid theater, which celebrated its hundredth birthday in 1997, is the legacy of rich coffee barons, who levied a tax on every bag of beans to pay for it. In the national museum a mural symbolizes the harvest and export of the crop which, as is often said, made Costa Rica great. To a large extent, the country's future was determined by nineteenth-century coffee barons, while those who established coffee plantations in neighboring Nicaragua and Guatemala were Costa Ricans. The coffee sector is still the country's biggest employer, and after tourism and bananas represents the third largest source of foreign currency, accounting for eleven per cent of exports in 1996. Income from coffee fluctuates heavily, however, depending on the movement of prices on the world market. In 1996 coffee brought in \$378 million, for instance, while in 1986 a much smaller volume of exports earned \$392 million.

The economic importance of coffee has declined over recent years as other sectors have expanded, and the time when coffee and bananas alone determined the fate of the national economy is definitely past. In 1994, after frost had damaged plantations in Brazil, the export value of coffee rose sharply following years of low prices. The government's response to rising prices was to levy a high export tax, a move which enraged producers. In January 1995 some 3,000 coffee farmers took to the streets in San José, demanding reductions in the taxes and levies on coffee production (10 per cent) and exports (eighteen per cent). President Figueres, himself the owner of a coffee plantation, capitulated and both taxes were dropped, in return for an agreement on income tax and a lower selling price for coffee supplied to the domestic market.

The precarious reliance of the coffee sector on fluctuating international prices was revealed at the beginning of 1995 when prices plummeted because of a glut on the world market. Most Central American countries, including Costa Rica, decided to hold back twenty per cent of exports in reserve in an attempt to force up prices. In July that year Colombia and the Central American countries even temporarily suspended the whole of their exports. The policy of export retention has been regulated by the Association of Coffee Producing Countries (ACPC), of which Costa Rica is a member, which allots quotas to individual countries. By 1997, prices had recovered again, thanks to low stocks in Brazil and strikes in Colombia, and Costa Rica urged the ACPC, without success, to lift its export quotas and allow producers to capitalize on high prices.

Despite some progress made by the ACPC, pricing problems show no sign of being solved as long as there is no new international coffee agreement between coffee-producing and coffee-consuming countries. The International Coffee Agreement lapsed in 1989 when producer countries, particularly Indonesia and Brazil, could not agree between themselves over fixing export levels. Until 1989 the worst price fluctuations on the world market could be prevented by harmonizing supply and demand to some extent, but subsequently a free-trade system has existed, with no price guarantees in force.

Cooperatives

Costa Rica has a large number of small and medium-size coffee farmers who make use of seasonal workers or at harvest time sub-contract their own employees to the big companies. These farmers are usually organized in cooperatives, where the Instituto del Café (ICAFE) plays an important role. First established by the government in the 1930s to protect small farmers from predatory coffee barons, ICAFE now regulates the whole national coffee trade, ruling on prices to be paid by exporters to producers. It has long been earmarked for privatization.

The government has been able to compensate for regular price collapses in the last few decades by considerably raising levels of production. This has been largely the result of technological innovation; mainly after 1950, new varieties were introduced, disease was combated more effectively, there were better fertilizing methods, and farmers made use of more modern irrigation technology. The cooperatives have played an important role in all such advances. Export figures reveal the extent of production growth: in 1861 Costa Rica exported 45,000 kilos/100,000 pounds of coffee, in 1975 190 million, in 1980 220 million, and in 1990 some 340 million pounds.

Industrialization

Costa Rica's economic problems began in the 1970s when government spending began to get out of hand. Between 1940 and 1978 public services and the infrastructure expanded at a dramatic rate as the state built new roads, bridges, port facilities, and waterworks and invested heavily in education and health care. A plethora of state companies and government departments provided legions of jobs. At the beginning of the 1940s President Rafael Angel Calderón had begun the practice of government intervention and under successive social-democratic PLN governments state influence increased even further. To finance the growth of the state sector, governments drew on the banking sector, which had been nationalized in 1948, hence covering budget deficits and creating a large domestic debt. While the Costa Rican model achieved real successes in terms of social peace, a real process of industrialization did not materialize. Agriculture remained the mainstay of the economy, fueling GDP growth rates between 1950 and 1980 of a few percentage points per year. Steady economic growth occurred in part thanks to the enormous increase in land available for agriculture. At the beginning of the 1950s Costa Rican farmers were only working a fifth of their national territory; by 1973, 73 per cent of the land was under cultivation, and it was not until the end of the 1970s that this expansion came to a halt. In the meantime, jobs in agriculture had fallen drastically. In 1950 50 per cent of the population were still active in the agricultural sector; in 1993 just over fifteen per cent worked in farming.

In terms of employment, the greatest growth area was government itself. In 1950 six per cent of workers were on the state payroll; in 1980 one in five of those in work was employed in the public sector.

Import Substitution

Until recently Costa Rica's economy depended overwhelmingly on the export of agricultural products such as coffee, bananas, and sugar. Recurring experiences of fluctuating prices and natural disasters had long exposed the economy's vulnerability, and during the 1950s the notion of reducing dependence on commodities became widespread. Diversification became the watchword, both in Costa Rica and elsewhere, and Costa Rica embraced the thinking of the UN organization, the Economic Commission for Latin America (CEPAL), which advocated industrialization as a way of escaping over-dependence on primary commodities.

The initiatives needed to get such industrialization off the ground were developed with other countries in the region. The Central American Common Market (MCCA) was established in 1960, in which Guatemala, Honduras, El Salvador, Nicaragua, and Costa Rica maintained a joint export tariff and developed regional free trade. Huge import tariffs were imposed on industrial products coming from outside Central America, while low levies were applied to the raw materials necessary to manufacture these products locally. Known as import substitution, the strategy of replacing industrial imports by domestic production was a seasoned recipe in Latin America in the 1960s and 1970s. Attracted by very favorable tax regulations, a large number of North American companies established themselves in

Cattle market in Guanacaste *Rob Rietvelt, B&U Int.Picture Service*

Central America. Generating high growth rates and a spectacular increase in regional trade, the MCCA appeared to be a success story.

By the end of the 1970s, however, the MCCA was facing disintegration and the import substitution model was running out of steam. Industrial production had concentrated too strongly on the domestic and Central American markets, the former being too small and the latter too politically volatile. The 1969 "Soccer War" between El Salvador and Honduras and civil wars in El Salvador and Nicaragua were hardly conducive to stable markets and mutual trade. As Central America slipped further into political turbulence, the MCCA disintegrated. Import substitution also fell into disfavor as Costa Rica spent more importing raw materials and machinery than it earned through industrial exports. The tax advantages enjoyed by the new industries were also a drain on the state exchequer, creating a structural deficit in the balance of payments and forcing successive governments into covering their spending with loans. The great debt crisis began to take shape; the oil price rise of 1973 and the sharp increase in state-sector spending accelerated its impact.

Cattle Farming

Another strategy for reducing dependence on coffee and bananas was to widen the country's range of export products, and from the 1950s onwards the government and banks deliberately promoted cattle farming as an export alternative. Cattle farming is concentrated mainly in the northern province of Guanacaste, where ranches account for some 70 per cent of the total land available for agriculture. Beef was for a long time the third most important export product after bananas and coffee, but it has never accounted for more than nine per cent of total exports.

Influenced by the steady increase in the price of meat, the already extensive cattle farming sector experienced vigorous growth in the 1960s. Beef exports trebled between 1960 and 1978, most exported as frozen meat to the United States. Some of this meat then returned to Costa Rica in the shape of hamburgers. Yet despite export growth, the expansion of cattle farming had significant downsides. Enormous areas of forest had to be cleared for the cattle ranches, and over-grazing was responsible for soil erosion on a huge scale. The sector is the exclusive fiefdom of large landowners and provides very few jobs.

Non-Traditional Exports

It is only during the last two decades that the Costa Rican economy has really diversified significantly, in particular through the rise of the non-traditional sector and tourism. The development of non-traditional exports has been one of the Costa Rican economy's most publicized success stories, with the government giving hefty subsidies from the early 1980s to any company exporting anything other than coffee, bananas, meat, sugar, or cocoa. This is why foreign companies have flocked to Costa Rica, attracted by tax breaks and other incentives and why Costa Rica now exports plastics, wood, confectionery, dairy products, alcohol from cane sugar, textiles, flowers, coconuts, pharmaceutical products, rubber bands, ornamental plants, pineapples, tuna fish, and jewelry. Although each product generates relatively low export revenue, taken together non-traditional exports accounted for as much as 60 per cent of total export value by 1994 (in 1980 the figure was still only ten per cent).

The boom in non-traditional exports has encompassed cut flowers, melons, and gold jewelry, but it is the textile industry which during the last ten years has experienced the most spectacular growth. Ten years ago there was hardly any such sector in Costa Rica, yet now it accounts for 50,000 jobs and exports women's apparel worth $50 million annually to the United States. Whether this will remain the case, however, is now uncertain. The coming into effect on January 1, 1994 of the North American Free Trade Agreement (NAFTA) between the U.S., Canada, and Mexico seems to have had a detrimental effect on Costa Rican textiles, and according to Miguel Schyfter, chairman of the Chamber of Industry, Costa Rica has had difficulty competing with Mexico, which now has free access

COSTA RICA

The colors blue (faith and justice) and white (purity and fairness) are reminiscent of the flag of the Central American Federation of which Costa Rica was a member between 1821 and 1838. When in 1848 the last links were severed, the present flag was introduced. The red band (red as the symbol for blood) incorporating (occasionally) the State Arms, was a tribute to the 1848 revolution in Europe.

(Vlaggen Dokumentatie Centrum Nederland)

An expedition through the rainforest. Tourism is currently Costa Rica's most important source of foreign currency. Its natural wealth offers nature lovers an unrivaled choice of flowers, animals and spectacular landscapes.

(Sygma)

The Irazú Volcano National Park, one of many protected areas which cover a quarter of the country.

(B&U International Picture Service/ Rob Rietvelt)

For a long time bananas were Costa Rica's principal source of foreign currency. Only during the last fifteen years has manufacturing taken an increasing share of exports and the tourist trade become more important. The banana bunches grow in plastic sacks attached to the trees. These protect the fruit against insects and also retain the sun's heat during tropical rainstorms.

(B&U International Picture Service/3F Productions Uithoorn)

The banana "hands" are packed into crates for export.

(Tjabel Daling)

When the bunches of bananas are ripe they are transported to the plantation's factory buildings. Cable transport is now taking over this job from the narrow-gauge railroads.

(Tjabel Daling)

In the "factory" the bunches are cut into hands. They are then washed in huge tanks.

(Tjabel Daling)

The crates go into huge cold-storage containers. These are then transported by trucks and trains to the ports and from there to the markets of North America and Europe. The cultivation, transport and marketing of Costa Rican bananas is in the hands of three multinational companies: Chiquita Brands, Standard Fruit/Dole, and Del Monte.

(B&U International Picture Service/3F Productions Uithoorn)

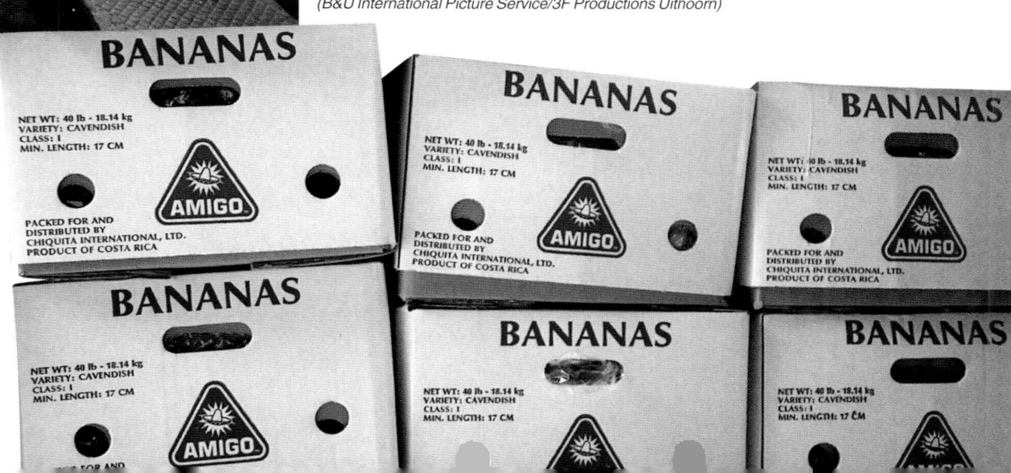

Picking ripe coffee berries. In the nineteenth century coffee was the basis of Costa Rica's prosperity. The center of the coffee-growing region is the high Meseta Central, the area around San José with its temperate climate. For many small farmers coffee is an important source of income.

(B&U International Picture Service/ 3F Productions Uithoorn)

The coffee berries go to a factory which is usually owned by a cooperative. The berries are washed and peeled, after which the beans are laid out in the sun to dry. They have to be turned regularly. The dried beans are then bagged up for export.

(Tjabel Daling)

to the huge American market. Textile exports from Costa Rica had already fallen in the first six months of 1994 by ten per cent, and subsequent protectionist measures by the U.S. have further damaged the Costa Rican industry. As it seems unlikely that the Central America states will be able to join NAFTA in the near future, it is probable that textile factories will shelve their expansion plans. Other experts point out that some textile companies have already transferred their production to Mexico.

The growth of the textile sector has been closely linked to the emergence of *maquiladora* industry, the industrial finishing of products which have been part-manufactured in other countries (usually the U.S.). Foreign companies provide the capital, the raw materials, the machinery, and the technology; Costa Rica provides the workforce and the factory premises for processing the finished products. Some *maquila* factories are situated in purpose-built free trade zones, which operate as low-wage enclaves where a largely female workforce assemble electronic goods or garments for export to the U.S. By the mid-1990s it was estimated that 134 companies were present in Costa Rica's eight free trade zones, employing nearly 20,000 workers.

Transnational Costa Rica

"Accompanying the growth of agricultural exports, aggressive penetration of foreign capital has given rise to the heralded 'transnationalization of Costa Rican agriculture.' Foreign presence in agroindustry is indeed impressive: Two transnational corporations — British American Tobacco and Philip Morris — control tobacco production and processing. Del Monte controls most pineapple, mango, papaya, chayote, and lemon exports. Including bananas, Del Monte's agroexports represent nine per cent of the country's total export production. United Brands controls palm oil production and exports, as well as the domestic production of margarine and shortening. Approximately 80 per cent of fern exports, 50 per cent of cut flower production, and 40 per cent of macadamia nut exports are controlled by foreign investors.

Foreign capital has also entered the industrial sector, especially through the Temporary Admission [*maquila*] and Free Trade Zone programs. In many cases foreign investment takes the form of the purchase of locally owned companies. More than 50 years after its establishment, the chocolate factory 'El Gallito' (the Little Rooster), a virtual symbol of Costa Rican nationalism, was acquired by the Philip Morris Company. Another Costa Rican property, Monpik Ice Cream, was recently bought jointly by the Mexican firm Quant Mexico, the Guatemalan firm Helados Mariposa, and Costa Rican associates. CPC International bought the Lizano sauces factory, another national symbol, and acquired the rights to Chiquita Brands and Numar to produce Clover and Hellman's mayonnaise. Foreign transnationals have established their presence in the metals and machinery industries as well."

Silvia Lara, Tom Barry and Peter Simonson, *Inside Costa Rica*, 1995

Tourism

In 1995 some 700,000 tourists visited Costa Rica, and with a total value of $661 million that year, this sector has now become Costa Rica's main source of income. Some estimates assume that by 2000 the number of visitors will have overtaken the two million mark. Between 1988 and 1993 annual revenue increased by an average of 25 per cent, but at the beginning of 1995 entrepreneurs in the tourist sector began to express concern for the first time about falling arrivals. After a decade of spectacular growth, investment, and unusually high room occupancy rates, there were reports of many empty hotels on the Caribbean coast. By 1997 tourism had still not recovered substantially, and growth in 1997 was less than one per cent after a sharp fall in 1996.

Robberies, the murder of an American tourist, the rape of two Canadian women at the end of 1994, and above all the abduction (on New Year's Day 1996) of a German woman tourist and a Swiss guide, caused a huge shock wave. An armed gang demanded a ransom of $1 million, and the hostages were only freed at the beginning of March after the ransom was paid. In the aftermath of the incident American and Canadian embassies warned their citizens of the dangers of visiting Costa Rica; 80 percent of tourists come from these two countries. The Costa Rican government fears that the country is losing its reputation as the safest destination in the region and has taken extra security precautions, especially near the border with Nicaragua. Government plans to increase substantially entry fees to the national parks have also deterred tourists, according to some local operators, and they also blame competition from countries such as Mexico and Cuba.

NAFTA and Regional Collaboration

Costa Rica's attempt to diversify its economy has also entailed a concerted bid to expand its range of markets. On January 1, 1995 the Figueres government signed a free trade accord with Mexico, which provides for 87 per cent of the products of either country being imported without quotas or tariffs. The aim is to achieve full free trade within fifteen years. This treaty is potentially very important for Costa Rica in that it now opens a potential market of almost 100 million Mexicans for some 5,000 products. Advocates of the treaty believe that within five years Costa Rica will be in a position to export goods to Mexico to the value of $250 million, an immense difference compared with the $17 million of exports in 1992. Opponents of the treaty are primarily afraid of cheap Mexican imports. "We shall have to see what happens," was the reaction of the Minister of Trade, José Rossi, in January 1995. "Don't ask me what we can consume. Ask me what we can export." Manufacturers who import raw materials on

Costa Rica is trying to create a "green" image: the Costa Rican clothes manufacturer J&B uses the trade name *ecological* for its products.

Courtesy of Tjabel Daling

a large scale are expected to benefit from the treaty, since until recently they had to pay a five per cent import duty. Raw materials such as synthetic resin, chemicals, and metals can now be imported duty-free.

San José does not wish to wait until 2005 when all Latin American countries will be able to join NAFTA. President Figueres has argued on a number of occasions that Central American countries should enjoy parity with Mexico and that membership of NAFTA should be made easier. So far his appeals have been ignored in the United States and Canada, where powerful textile lobbies are opposed to further concessions to Central America. And indeed, not everybody in Costa Rica is entirely enthusiastic about NAFTA. Many businessmen are afraid of a further influx of cheap imports, and workers and environmentalists have raised broader fears.

Costa Rica is also a supporter of stronger economic integration with its neighbors and is an active member of the Central American Common Market which was revived in 1987. Talks with leaders of the Caribbean Common Market (CARICOM), the Mercosur trade bloc (Argentina, Brazil, Uruguay, and Paraguay), and Chile suggest that a series of free-trade agreements may soon take place. Joint regional initiatives have also attracted funding from the European Union and Taiwan as well as the Inter-American Development Bank. But lingering suspicions and nationalist sentiment remain. A recent proposal by El Salvador for a single Central American currency and total free trade within five years was regarded by many Costa Rican politicians and businessmen going too far down the road of integration.

3 SOCIETY: FIRST WORLD, THIRD WORLD

Social Provision

In comparison with its neighbors, Costa Rica has proper legislation for social provision, an excellent education system, and a good health service. The abolition of the army made it possible to make huge investments in sectors such as education and health, meaning that according to figures published by the United Nations, 97 per cent of the population have access to health care (in the 1960s the figure was only fifteen per cent). About 92 per cent of *Ticos* have access to clean water, while average life expectancy in Costa Rica is a "first world" 76. Infant mortality is low at 14 per 1,000, and today's Costa Rican families average only two or three children. In 1990 Costa Rica was declared by the UN to be the developing country with the highest index of social development.

The situation in neighboring countries is altogether less rosy. In El Salvador and Guatemala, for instance, only 47 and 62 per cent respectively of the population have access to clean water. In the other Central American republics life expectancy is on average ten years lower (with the exception of Panama). The average income of a Nicaraguan is only one-sixth that of a Costa Rican; in El Salvador and Guatemala it is about half. Only Panama approaches Costa Rica in these indices of prosperity.

Health care

The Costa Rican Fund for Social Security (CCSS) plays a central role in the health service system. The fund was established in 1941 and manages dozens of hospitals and some 130 outpatient clinics. The principal source of income for the CCSS is obligatory employee insurance, whereby workers pay eight per cent of their salary and the employer adds another ten per cent of the wage. For a long time employers and the unemployed could not be insured through the fund, but now a form of voluntary insurance is available. Employers, however, frequently make use of private clinics, and small farmers have in fact usually made an arrangement with the CCSS.

During recent years the fund has become more active in areas such as information, education and prevention. Wide-scale public information campaigns are being conducted in order to disseminate information about healthy lifestyles and diet, often in close collaboration with schools. In addition to the CCSS, the Ministry of Health operates its own programs, and services, for example relating to birth control, drug problems, and the control of infectious diseases.

Although the standard of health care is very high indeed, complaints about state hospitals are legion: long waiting periods for treatment by medical specialists, preference given to patients who pay extra, poor service, corruption and strikes at national hospitals, where patients are the victims. In 1994 the Chairman of the CCSS, Dr. Alvaro Salas Chaves, acknowledged the complaints and early in 1995 President Figueres himself spoke about the "crisis in the health service" and the deterioration in the level of care in state hospitals. The government's main concern, he said, was that in the last few years diseases have begun to occur which were thought to have been eradicated from Costa Rica, such as malaria, measles, cholera, and dengue. A scandal in 1996, when cancer patients received dangerously high doses of radiation, increased concerns, with one newspaper editorializing: "The sad truth is that the radiation tragedy is only the most extreme symptom of a general trend … Anyone who has had to make use of the country's hospitals can attest to difficult conditions facing medical professionals who are overwhelmed, overworked, and underpaid as the country's economic difficulties have caused budget-slashing across the board."

AIDS does not appear to occur on any large scale in Costa Rica although there is a dearth of reliable statistics on the subject. In September 1995 the Ministry of Health reported 851 cases of HIV infection to the World Health Organization (WHO). According to experts, the real figures are much higher, and at the end of 1994 WHO estimated the number of HIV-infected adults at approximately 9,000. Most of those affected are homosexual men, but although the number of female AIDS patients is relatively small, it is in fact gradually increasing. A significant cause is the *machismo* of many Costa Rican males. As a 36-year-old HIV-positive woman from a slum area in San José said in an interview, "We never ever used condoms. My husband was totally against it."

The government broadcasts television and cinema "commercials" advising people to use condoms. There is an AIDS telephone hotline, and with financial support from European development agencies health service workers provide advice and information. Prostitutes and women's groups are provided with techniques for encouraging the use of condoms.

Education

What is true of the health service is also true of education. Compared with neighboring countries, the level of education is high and the government invests heavily in the sector. Costa Rica was one of the first countries in the world to enshrine in its constitution that education should be free and compulsory.

According to official figures, 93 per cent of the population are able to read and write, meaning that Costa Rica stands head and shoulders above its neighbors, among whom both Panama (88 per cent) and Nicaragua (81 per cent) score lower while El Salvador and Honduras (both at 73 per cent) and Guatemala (55 per cent) are even further behind. But the education system in Costa Rica also has its weaknesses, and the much-repeated slogan "more teachers than soldiers" needs to some extent to be put in context.

University for Peace

A country without an army; a Nobel Peace Prize for President Arias. Where more suitable than Costa Rica for the establishment of a University for Peace?

The University for Peace in San José was the initiative of President Rodrigo Carazo (1978-82). The aim is to encourage the teaching of peace in universities and educational institutions throughout the world, and the university develops projects for peace education, ecology, human rights, and conflict resolution on behalf of churches, trade unions, and other institutions. At about the same time as the University for Peace was being built, the Inter-American Court of Human Rights and the Inter-American Institute for Human Rights were established in Costa Rica. The presence of the two foundations confirms Costa Ricans' image of their country as a leader in the sphere of human rights, peace, and democracy.

When in late 1994 the veteran communist, Manuel Mora, died, President Figueres declared himself saddened by the fact that many younger people had never heard of Mora. "There really is something wrong with our education system," he admitted. Eduardo Doryan, minister of Education, in a recent interview with the populist newspaper *Al Día*, acknowledged the commonly voiced criticism of education in Costa Rica that it concentrates too much on theoretical knowledge instead of research and practical application. Critics of the system also claim that the national syllabus is out of date and too many teachers are insufficiently trained.

Other problems are the large numbers of pupils who drop out before completing their education, a shortage of classrooms, teachers' low pay, and pressure put on the system by very high subscription rates. Some primary school classes have more than 40 children, and large numbers of applications for university places are, according to critics, leading to a lowering of academic standards.

Teachers often feel overburdened and suffer from stress. If they are absent they are not usually replaced, meaning that the children are sent home. *La Nación* newspaper reported in 1995 that almost a third of the total number of teachers were ill on average three weeks a year, or at least they were reporting sick. Teachers also complain about lack of status, inadequate resources, and overcrowded classrooms, which are often shared by two classes at the same time.

AIDS warning on hoarding. The text reads: She gets her eyes from her mother, her nose from her father and the AIDS virus from both of them. Protect your child from AIDS, be faithful to your partner.

Tjabel Daling

In 1997 education swallowed up more than a fifth (22 per cent) of the total government budget, a rise on the previous year's figure of 26.8 per cent. By far the greatest single item in the education budget is teachers' salaries.

Regional and Social Inequality

The expansion of extensive cattle farming and large-scale modern agriculture in the last few decades has resulted in both a concentration of land-ownership and dwindling job opportunities in rural areas. The outcome has been a widespread migration of rural Costa Ricans to the city. A good 50 per cent of the population now live in or around the capital, San José, and more than two-thirds in the Meseta Central, the Central Plateau, where three of the four other main urban areas are situated: Alajuela, Heredia, and Cartago, the only other city of importance being Puerto Limón.

"Costa Rica is the Meseta Central, and the Meseta Central is Costa Rica," says Iván Molina Jiménez, a historian and demographer at the Universidad de Costa Rica. The primacy of the capital and surrounding region takes many forms: the cultural, social, and medical facilities are best in the center of the country, particularly in the San José conurbation. This is where most of state budget is allocated, this is where most industry is located, where the government institutions, the best educational institutes, and the most hospital beds are to be found. The Central Plateau also has the best infrastructure and communication network with other parts of the country.

In the rural areas of the coastal regions and Guanacaste, on the other hand, unemployment is much higher and illiteracy statistics are less impressive. The supply of drinking water and health services leaves much to be desired, and there is a greater incidence of infectious diseases. Compared with the country's central region, community facilities are also scarce and under-funded. The government is attempting to reduce regional inequality through the setting up of free trade zones in places such as

Puntarenas and Golfito. Foreign companies which want to establish themselves and create jobs in depressed areas are attracted by state subsidies and inducements which include large tax concessions.

Urban Migration

The government has tried to put a brake on migration from the countryside to the city but without real success. In 1960 some 65 per cent of the population lived in the countryside, a figure which had dropped to less than 50 per cent in 1980 and is expected to fall even further in the next century.

One of the causes of rural-urban migration has been the precarious existence of many farmers with land holdings which are far too small to be viable. In 1962 the government established the Lands and Colonization Institute (ITCO) in order to deal with the problem of unequal land distribution. The organization bought up land on behalf of landless peasants, particularly in the thinly-populated region of Guanacaste. Eighteen years later 3,000 families had taken possession of 180,000 acres through the ITCO, about two per cent of the total area available for agriculture.

The ITCO's successor, the Institute for Agrarian Development (IDA), has the same objectives, but has not brought about any extensive land reform either. Some experts argue that it is doubtful whether Costa Rica now needs land reform in any case. Many small peasant farmers have now built a new life in the city, abandoning agriculture altogether. The IDA has improved the position of those smallholders who have remained in the countryside by setting up agricultural cooperatives. Yet despite such improvements, there remains a relatively small group of very poor peasant farmers. A study dating from 1973 showed that five per cent of agricultural concerns, particularly banana plantations and cattle ranches, accounted for 55 per cent of arable land, and the growth of non-traditional exports has worsened this land concentration. The most vulnerable groups in the countryside are small tenant farmers and agricultural workers.

Other sectors of society are also the victims of economic inequality, although this is less acute than in neighboring countries. In 1989 the richest twenty per cent of Costa Ricans accounted for 51 per cent of the national income, the poorest twenty per cent taking only four per cent. (For Guatemala the corresponding figures were 63 and 2 per cent, for Nicaragua 55 and 5 per cent, and for Panama 60 and 2 per cent.). What is most remarkable in Costa Rica's distribution of income, however, is the considerable size of the middle classes. As Richard Biesanz comments in *The Costa Ricans*: "The growth of the middle classes [in recent decades] shows that considerable social mobility exists in Costa Rica."

Slum dwelling on the outskirts of San José. About a quarter of Costa Rica's population lives below the nationally established poverty level.

B&U Int. Picture Service/3F Prod.

Poverty

The economic crisis and the adjustment following the debt crisis of the 1980s have revealed increasing poverty in Costa Rican society. During the last ten years the quality of education and medical care have deteriorated, with only the rich escaping a general decline in provision through access to private schools and hospitals. About a quarter of Costa Ricans currently live below the nationally determined poverty line. There is an appalling shortage of housing, and in 2000 it is estimated that there will be a shortfall of 125,000 homes. Various presidents have promised to build tens of thousands of houses but in practice have been unable to fulfill such pledges.

Rural poverty has a nationwide knock-on effect. In urban centers single-parent families, poorly educated migrants, and those made redundant by retrenchment policies face a range of hardships and risks. This is particularly obvious in San José where many people take refuge in the informal sector (typically as shoe-shiners and street traders) and where hundreds of homeless children live on the streets, sniffing glue or using highly addictive crack cocaine. According to official figures, about 9,000 women work in Costa Rica as prostitutes, often forced to do so by economic circumstances, and these include many minors.

Ethnicity and Identity

As opposed to many other Latin American countries Costa Rica has a highly homogeneous population, about 97 per cent of people being of white (Spanish and Italian) or mixed Spanish-Indian descent. Black Costa Ricans and indigenous people make up small minorities, while approximately ten per cent of the present population comes from Nicaragua.

In 1996 Costa Rica's population stood at 3.4 million inhabitants. Between 1970 and 1980 annual population growth was 2.8 per cent; slowing down to 2.3 per cent in the period 1990-5. Costa Rica has the lowest birth and death rates in Central America. The decline in natural population growth is in part offset by continuing immigration from Nicaragua, and it is estimated that there will be 3.7 million Ticos by 2000.

Costa Ricans have a strong sense of national identity (some would say superiority), and Ticos make it very clear that they have little in common with other Central American nations. They look "whiter" and are generally more materialistic and individualist in outlook than the inhabitants of neighboring countries. A general fondness for all things American means that the average Costa Rican looks to the United States for a role model.

Blacks

Most black Costa Ricans are the descendants of immigrants from the Caribbean, particularly Jamaica, and are culturally closer to the English-speaking islands than to Hispanic Central America. In the nineteenth century their forebears were recruited to work on laying the railway line between San José and the Caribbean coast; and many later found work on the nearby banana and cocoa plantations. Since the 1949 constitution, the black population along the Atlantic coast has enjoyed the same rights as other Costa Ricans but their economic situation still leaves much to be desired. Many blacks complain that the government neglects the area where the majority of them live, the Talamanca region in the province of Limón.

For years Costa Rica's black population has faced discrimination. When the U.S. banana companies left the Atlantic region in 1934 because of the outbreak of Panama banana disease and relocated in the lowlands along the Pacific (in the neighborhood of Golfito), their black workers were not allowed to go with them, as President Jiménez expressly forbade the companies to employ "*gente de color*." If the black population left the eastern section of the Caribbean coast, according to Jiménez, the country's "racial balance" would be threatened.

Until relatively recently, the black minority has remained largely separate from mainstream Costa Rican society, and at the beginning of the twentieth century migrants from Jamaica avoided assimilation. They often felt

The people of Limón, a mural by Guadelupe Alvarez *Tjabel Daling*

themselves to be superior to the Indians and mixed-race mestizos, since many of the blacks who worked on the United Fruit Company banana plantations were able to read and write, whereas the great majority of mestizos were illiterate. In his book *A Folk-History of Costa Rica's Talamanca's Coast*, Paul Rodman, himself of Jamaican descent, describes the resulting tensions:

The Jamaicans believed that they were only in Costa Rica to earn money and then go home again. But only a few did go home. Those who had money decided that it was worth staying there and those who had earned nothing couldn't go back. Most Jamaicans did not want to mix with the Spaniards (mestizos), apart from a few exceptions. The Jamaicans looked on the mestizos as inferior and dirty. There was hatred and envy between the two groups. Fights were always breaking out on pay-day.

Rodman, the son of a contract worker on the Panama Canal, believed that United Fruit took maximum advantage from such ethnic divisions, operating a "divide-and-rule" policy. Usually it was black workers who organized strikes for better wages and living conditions on the plantations of the "Company," encouraged by the Universal Negro Improvement Association (UNIA) of Marcus Garvey. Jamaica-born Garvey first visited Costa Rica in 1909, and his experience of the deplorable conditions on the banana plantations was instrumental in his founding of the UNIA in 1919 and his life-long struggle for black emancipation.

During the strikes of 1913 and 1918 United Fruit called on police and white strike-breakers to intimidate the plantation workers, and violent clashes resulted. Hundreds of thousands of blacks were sacked, evicted from their company barracks, and in many cases their possessions and garden plots were destroyed.

Indians

Optimistic estimates suggest that there are currently 30,000 Indians (*indígenas*) living in Costa Rica, but pessimists put the figure at fewer than 10,000. Most live in the Talamanca region. The two largest Indian groupings are the Cabécares and the Bribrí, who, more actively than other Indian groups, are trying to preserve their own way of life, their culture and their language. This, according to an elderly female inhabitant of the Kéköldi reservation on the Atlantic coast where Bribrí and Cabécares live, is not easy:

I hope that we shall always remember our own languages, but that is difficult. Many younger people do not want to speak our languages any longer. They all speak Spanish and are ashamed of their own language. But how is it possible that the black population here speaks English and nobody criticizes them while we are ashamed to speak our own language? Sib [an indigenous divinity] gave us these languages. It would be a great cause for sorrow if we lost them.

Indigenous history over the last hundred years can be best summed up in terms of official indifference. For most of the twentieth century politicians and society were hardly aware of the existence of indigenous groups and it was only a few years ago that Indians were given full civil rights. In 1990 Guaymi Indians in San José were protesting that they still did not possess identity cards (*cédulas*). Without a *cédula* one cannot vote, borrow money, or use any of the state health care facilities.

Identity Under Threat

The majority of Indians live in special reservation areas (6.3 per cent of the national territory), but their land (and formally they do not own the land) is increasingly threatened by outside forces, including poachers, woodcutters, mining companies, landless peasants, and state plans for hydro-electric power stations. Their pitiable socio-economic situation forces many Indians to sell their small piece of land. In a pastoral letter the Catholic Church has criticized anti-indigenous discrimination, the bishops expressing their concerns about mining projects in Indian territory. Eco-tourism would, they said, reduce the Indians to "archaeological tourist attractions." Complaining that indigenous communities "are becoming slaves to the new investors," the church condemned the huge export-oriented agricultural businesses which have in some cases moved into reservation territory.

Indians and Indian organizations do, however, realize that they cannot isolate themselves from the outside world and sometimes they are quick to adapt to new developments. Tourists, for instance, are allowed in the reservations, albeit on a small scale. This is done in the knowledge that tourism is a potential new source of income and that the money can be used for the conservation of the rainforest.

Since 1950 the government has been carrying out a more or less conscious Indian policy, which critics attack, however, as being principally directed towards assimilation and too little towards the preservation of the Indians' own culture. The *Ley Indígena* of 1976, which was passed by parliament in the following year, established autonomous government structures in the 21 reservations which now exist. Three years previously, the National Commission for Indian Affairs (CONAI) had been set up, but many people saw this as a government-dominated body and in 1981 Indians formed their own organization, the Asociación Indígena Pablo Presbere.

In recent years a small-scale indigenous renaissance has taken place as Indian organizations have attempted to rediscover their identity and culture. The Guaymi, for example, who live in the border region of Panama, held an official coronation ceremony for their *cacique* or chief, this being the first occasion since 1930 that an Indian tribe had performed this solemn ceremony in Costa Rica. Since May 1995 the Cabécares and the Bribrí have had their own bank, the Banco Indígena de Talamanca. In the words of a spokesman from the Indian organization *Sejèktö* (The Indian Voice), "It is neither a private nor a state bank. It is a bank of and for Indians."

Nicaraguans

From the coffee and banana plantations to the slum districts of San José, Nicaraguan immigrants are omnipresent in modern Costa Rica. According to official figures, 400,000 Nicaraguans were living in Costa Rica in 1996, of whom some 300,000 are defined as illegal immigrants. They are all seeking work, work which either does not exist in their own country or is paid at a much lower rate. Although on average they earn only 60 per cent of what a Costa Rican would earn, Nicaraguans are eager to cross the border in search of a better life.

In 1995 the influx of migrants led to tension between San José and Managua, with Nicaragua accusing its southern neighbor of mistreating illegal immigrants and of systematic exploitation by Costa Rican employers. An agreement between President Figueres and Arnoldo Alemán of Nicaragua in May 1997 stipulated that Nicaraguans without work permits could be deported, but that employers should regulate conditions for those in recognized employment by paying social security contributions. Many fear that employers will ignore the ruling or simply fire "illegal" workers, since Nicaraguans are hired precisely to avoid such expenses and because "they do work which no Tico will ever do," as Agustín Castro, a columnist on the *Prensa Libre* newspaper, puts it. Public opinion is divided between anti-Nicaraguan prejudice and the belief that Nicaraguans are industrious, as well as cheap, workers.

Expatriates

Thousands of foreigners have settled in Costa Rica, many choosing the country as a place for their retirement home. The majority of so-called *pensionados* or *rentistas* (pensioners or retired) are Americans but there are also Germans, British, and other Europeans. For many years these wealthier immigrants enjoyed special privileges and were allowed to import their cars and many other items free of duty, but these incentives have now been withdrawn.

The foreigners include a large group of older single men hoping to find a young attractive woman to marry. The advertisements placed in *Tica Woman* by mostly American men suggest that dreams of exotic romance are commonplace, but stories in local newspapers frequently tell of women who are more interested in the money, house, and other possessions of the would-be husband.

Over the last few decades rich Americans have been buying up large areas of land and *fincas* (estates) in Costa Rica, often for the purpose of speculation. One such was the U.S. TV evangelist Jimmy Swaggert, who acquired several *haciendas* on the border with Nicaragua. Swaggert, who later caused his own spectacular downfall through his relationship with a prostitute in New Orleans, tried to spread his fundamentalist message through Central America from Guanacaste, while at the same time raising funds to support the armed struggle of the Contras against the Sandinistas in Nicaragua.

The relationship between some American land owners, who hardly spend any time on their land, and the Costa Rican government is not always cordial and this has occasionally affected official relations between Costa Rica and the U.S. Disputes almost always concern the expropriation of

One expatriate settled in Costa Rica and started an export business for orchids and other tropical plants

B&U Int. Picture Service/3F Prod.

land for establishing a national park, for instance, or for developing a region for tourism or the creation of an Indian reservation. Expropriated absentee landowners have complained that compensation provisions are non existent or ignored. The authorities in San José are normally unsympathetic, insisting that foreign land owners have acquired the land for a trifling sum and sometimes without legal title and then demand compensation. Land owners have also faced conflict with landless peasants and squatters (*precaristas*) who make use of the land in their absence.

Social Organization

Since the beginning of the 1980s the once-powerful trade union movement has lost much of its authority and influence, particularly because of the rise of *solidarismo*: the concept of worker-employer cooperation.

Solidarismo is a system in which employer and employees theoretically work together for shared aims of greater production and industrial harmony, seeing the company as an ethical as well as commercial entity. The first company union was set up in 1948 by the Costa Rican lawyer Alberto Marten Chavarria as an alternative to the communist-aligned trade unions and the idea of class confrontation. Employees and employers deposit an agreed sum from wages and profit into a fund from which workers can obtain cheap credit and access to medical and recreational facilities. The government and many companies actively encourage these associations as alternatives to collective bargaining and strikes.

A former U.S. ambassador to Costa Rica, Curtin Winsor, referred to this phenomenon as "perhaps the most original and significant ideological contribution of Latin America to the West." Not surprisingly, *solidarismo* is strongest in the private sector and among multinationals in particular: companies involved include Firestone, McDonalds, Coca-Cola, Pizza Hut, Del Monte, IBM, Standard Brands, and Colgate Palmolive. According to Winsor, the movement has its origins in "peace-loving Costa Rica" and has brought about stable labor relations and increased productivity.

The traditional trade union movement, on the other hand, claims that *solidarismo* undermines the independence of the trade union movement, with strong pressure exerted on employees to leave unions and to join associations. The International Association of Trade Unions believes that employers' interests prevail in *solidarismo* associations and that "company unions" discourage collective labor agreements and opportunities for strike action. Trade unions in the banana plantations, once among the country's most militant, have been severely weakened, with a negative impact on wages and conditions.

The Costa Rican Labor Code of 1988 has, according to critics, not only given preference to *solidarismo* over trade unions, but has also severely restricted the power of the "old" unions. The law stipulates, for instance, that a minimum of twenty workers is necessary for establishing a trade union in a workplace, while only five are needed for a *solidarista* union.

Despite the growth of *solidarismo* and considerable fragmentation between different unions, the labor movement succeeded in 1995 in organizing the biggest demonstrations Costa Rica's history, and the teachers' unions in particular are still able to mobilize their huge rank and file. Public-sector unions have been instrumental in forcing the Figueres government to slow the pace of its neo-liberal retrenchment policies, and industrial action has won other concessions in the areas of pensions and other rights.

Cooperatives

Cooperative associations of producers and consumers play an important role in Costa Rica, having expanded in the 1970s as part of the state's development strategy. They are active in various spheres such as agriculture, the services industry, and manufacturing, and they also function as savings and credit banks. The social-democratic governments of Daniel Odúber, Luis Alberto Monge and Oscar Arias Sánchez gave particular impetus to cooperatives, viewing them as central in the "democratization of the economy."

The Monge administration enacted popular legislation through which peasant farmers or workers who wanted to set up a cooperative, but who did not have the financial resources to do so, could obtain a loan from the state. This policy proved very successful and the number of cooperatives grew very rapidly, as did the number of members, currently around 340,000.

The business of the savings and credit cooperatives is financial resourcing, and they offer their members favorable interest rates. Thanks to bulk purchasing, consumer cooperatives can offer their members all kinds of goods at cheaper prices. The industrial cooperatives are principally concerned with the processing of agricultural produce, a well-known example being the Dos Pinos milk factory. There are also cooperatives in the agricultural and services sector, the latter active in recreation, transport, housing, and electricity supply. Electricity cooperatives bring power to rural districts which the state-owned Costa Rican Electricity Institute (ICE) neglects. Agricultural cooperatives take rice, cattle, sugar, or coffee to the market for their members, meaning that better prices can be negotiated. They also bulk buy seeds, fertilizer, and machinery, meaning that "strength in numbers" ensures lower prices.

The Catholic Church

At least 90 per cent of Costa Ricans are Roman Catholics, at least in name, and although almost all Ticos say that they believe in God, most people are relaxed rather than fanatical about their religion. A Catholic philosopher once concluded that Costa Ricans' easy religious attitudes were part of what he termed their *a la gana* mentality: do what you feel like doing. The church's ideological role has been important in underpinning the country's social-democratic model, and critics have described it as paternalistic and conservative in its attitudes.

Fewer than twenty per cent of Costa Ricans attend mass regularly, and Sunday is rather more an occasion for the beach or other leisure pursuits. Many Ticos also adhere to the principle of *personalismo*; they go to church if they like the priest, and if they don't, they stay away. Women attend church more often then men, most males only going to church for baptisms, weddings, and funerals.

The saints often seem to play a bigger role in popular Catholicism than God; there is a statue of the Virgin Mary in almost every house and many a car dashboard carries an image of a saint. Every year on August 2 thousands of pilgrims from the whole of Central America attend the Cartago Basilica to revere the Virgen de los Angeles (the Madonna of the Angels), who has been the patron saint of Costa Rica since 1782. Many Ticos also believe in the world of *brujos*, magicians and witches.

Costa Rica numbers some 40,000 Protestants, and during the last ten years, as elsewhere in Latin America, evangelical churches have been very active and successful. Many people, particularly among poorer communities, have become members of one of the 115 sects which present their message of individual salvation with the help of U.S. resources.

Women's Movement

Miguel Schyfter, President of the National Chamber of Industry, once remarked that "sexual intimidation is part of the culture of our country." Since then new legislation has been enacted, providing for action to be taken against sexual harassment at work and in schools. Employers and heads of schools are now obliged to take action against sexual intimidation and to take preventive measures, while the Ministry of Labor checks to ensure that the measures are being carried out. In theory, the law applies equally to men and women, but in practice it will be woman principally who resort to it, even if in the macho culture of Costa Rica women are still often regarded as outside the law.

Various women's organizations insist that existing legislation does not go far enough and that there should be many more changes in the social relationships between men and women. In an estimated 30 to 40 per cent of families women are the victim of sexual violence, a problem which seems to be on the increase, and incest is also believed to be widespread. In spite of the emphasis placed on the family by the Catholic Church, stable family life remains elusive for many; divorce is common and between 40 and 50 per cent of births occur outside marriage, with the father unknown in one in five cases. Abortion is officially banned in Catholic Costa Rica unless the health of the woman is threatened, yet every year between 5,000 and 8,000 illegal abortions are carried out, according to a University of Costa Rica study.

The percentage of women in the labor force has increased enormously in the last few decades; in 1963 ten per cent of workers were women, in 1973 the figure had doubled, and has now reached almost 30 per cent. In some cases, individual women have succeeded in traditionally male preserves. Maureen Clarke, minister for internal affairs in President Figueres' cabinet, for example, was the country's first black woman to hold a ministerial post.

But generally women continue to play a subordinate role in political and social life, accounting for a mere fourteen per cent of all political posts and receiving only nineteen per cent of the national income. Women have less easy access to well-paid jobs than men and for the same work they are paid less, earning on average 86 per cent of what a man earns.

Unemployment among women is also higher; in 1992, 5.5 per cent of economically active women were without a job, whereas for men the figure was 3.5 per cent.

NGOs and Voluntary Organizations

Non-governmental organizations (NGOs) are thick on the ground in Costa Rica and are active in a broad field of issues. They have proliferated since the 1980s in particular, partly in response to deteriorating social conditions and partly because of Costa Rica's reputation for relative stability. Many NGOs are financed from abroad, particularly by the U.S. Agency for International Development (USAID), which has concentrated on relief to the sectors worst hit by structural adjustment. The environment is another important focal point, with NGOs providing environment education, taking on responsibility for recycling, promoting the interests of peasant farmers and Indians, or trying to promote "greener" production methods within banana plantations. Many students and volunteers from abroad are (temporarily) attached to these organizations and combine their work with a vacation in Costa Rica.

4 ENVIRONMENT AND ECO-TOURISM

Palm-fringed beaches, coral reefs, volcanoes and mountain ranges, a paradise of flora and fauna; when it comes to natural beauty, Costa Rica really has everything. About five per cent of all the animal and plant varieties which exist on earth are to be found in this small Central American country: 850 different kinds of bird, 220 species of reptile and amphibian, 209 species of mammal, 1,500 different trees, and 350,000 varieties of insects, spiders, and crustaceans.

At first sight, this natural wealth appears to be in safe hands. Some twelve per cent of the national territory is designated as national parks, where nature enjoys full official protection. The government eventually plans to extend the national parks, of which there are currently 35, to cover more than nineten per cent of the country. In addition, there are also a good number of buffer zones and forest, game, and biological reservations which are used for reforestation, environmental projects, and eco-tourism. Altogether, a quarter of Costa Rica's national territory is officially protected land in what is the best conservation system in Latin America.

Deforestation

Yet despite environmental legislation and planning, Costa Rica's natural resources are under threat, even in the national parks, where illegal tree-felling continues to take place. Although theoretically they are under state supervision, areas within the national parks still remain, legally at least, in private hands since the government has not bought the land. An influx of landless peasants into such marginal zones has caused widespread destruction of forests, and illicit tree-cutting is thought to have accounted for 80 per cent of forest losses in the early 1990s.

In Costa Rica the process of rainforest destruction has been the fastest in the whole of Latin America. In 1950, 72 per cent of the country consisted of forest; by 1973, the area had shrunk to 49 per cent, in 1978, 34 per cent, and in 1985, 26 per cent. If deforestation continues at this pace, shortly after the year 2000 there will be no more tropical forest, either dry forest, rainforest, or cloud forest, left at all.

It does seem, however, that the rate of forest destruction is gradually slowing. A few years ago an average of 100,000 acres of forest were being felled annually. By 1994 there was a net loss of 20,000 acres, after allowing for the planting of new trees; in 1995 the government claimed to have reduced the figure to 10,000 acres, insisting that by 1996 there was to be no further loss of forest.

The causes of massive deforestation over recent decades are legion. In the central and higher regions of Costa Rica, coffee growing has been responsible for the disappearance of large areas of jungle, and banana plantations have been pushing back forests in coastal areas on a huge scale since the beginning of the twentieth century. There is a great deal of money to be earned from tropical hardwood exports, while the promotion of cattle breeding by the government in response to North American demand has led to a massive expansion of grazing lands. Colonization projects for landless peasant farmers have also been sited in areas from which all forest first had to be cleared. Rapid population growth has also contributed to deforestation. In 1900, Costa Rica had a population of 300,000, rising to 1.8 million by 1972 and now standing at 3.2 million. Particularly in the Central Plateau region, urban sprawl has enveloped large areas of woodland. In recent years the increasing number of tourists has also had a deleterious effect on the environment.

Government Policy

Faced with a potential deforestation crisis, Costa Rican governments have adopted an active policy of environmental protection over the last decade. The Arias administration drafted a national conservation strategy in 1988, and many of its recommendations have been enacted. The state wants to buy up vulnerable natural areas which are still in the hands of private owners in an attempt to create buffer zones around the national parks. President Figueres has enthusiastically embraced the fashionable phrase "sustainable development" and has promised to build a "constructive alliance with nature." Pledging to plant 3.2 million trees before his period of office comes to an end in 1998, Figueres has insisted that "Costa Rica must become the first country in the world to plant more trees than it fells." In other words, a tree for every Costa Rican.

The government is also trying to take action against illegal logging. A reforestation program enables farmers and farmers' cooperatives to replant their fallow lands with technical help and sometimes financial assistance from the state. Loans are available for farmers who modernize their beef production along approved environmental lines and who are prepared to plant trees or environmentally friendly crops on part of their lands. To pay for such initiatives, the government has imposed a "green" tax on bananas, a carbon tax, and an electricity tax as an incentive for energy conservation. The World Bank and donor countries have also been receptive to funding rainforest conservation programs.

In the regional context, too, Costa Rica has sought to establish its credentials with regard to the environment. Figueres played a leading part

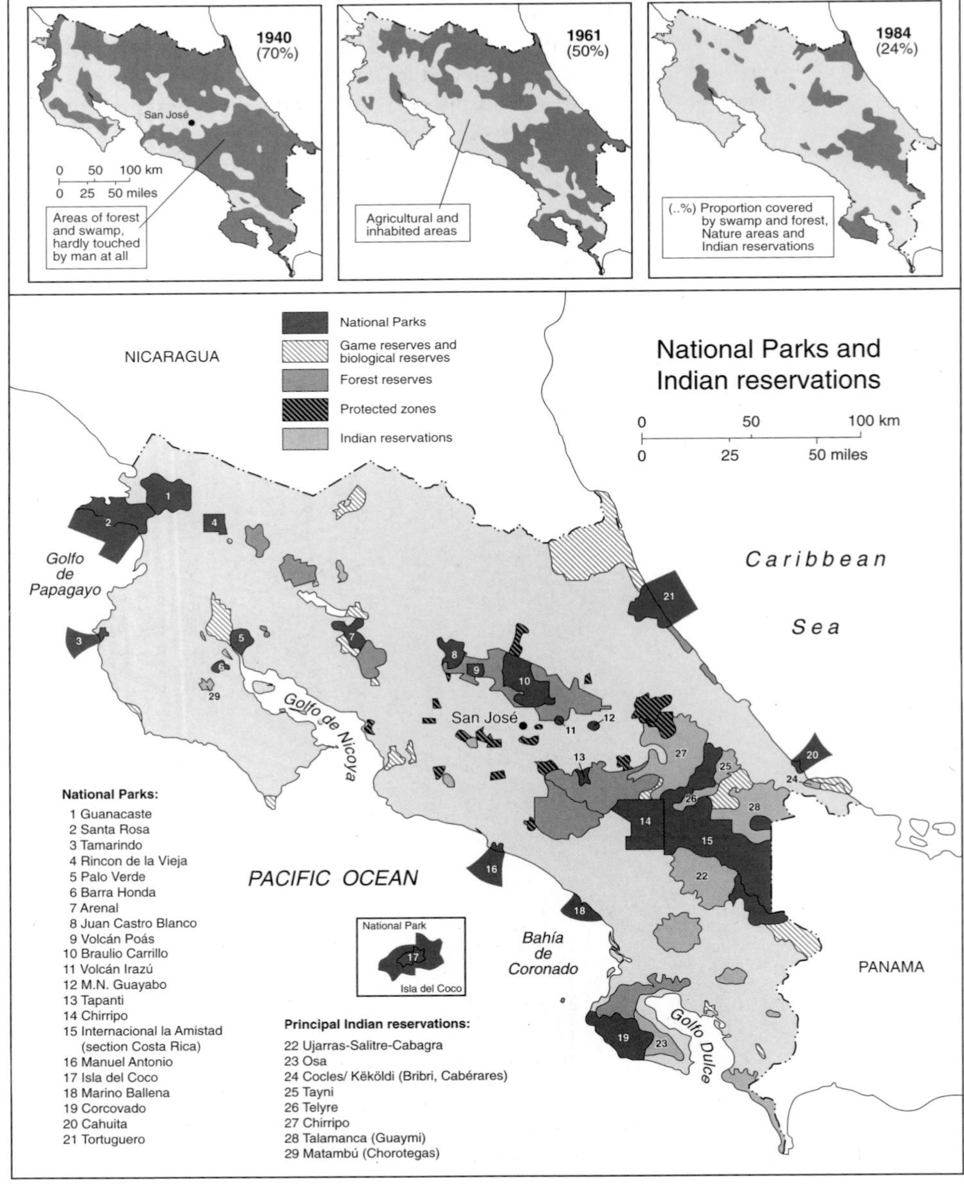

1940
(70%)
San José
0 50 100 km
0 25 50 miles
Areas of forest and swamp, hardly touched by man at all
1961
(50%)
Agricultural and inhabited areas
1984
(24%)
(..%) Proportion covered by swamp and forest, Nature areas and Indian reservations
National Parks
Game reserves and biological reserves
Forest reserves
Protected zones
Indian reservations
NICARAGUA
National Parks and Indian reservations
0 50 100 km
0 25 50 miles
Caribbean Sea
Golfo de Papagayo
Golfo de Nicoya
San José
PACIFIC OCEAN
National Park
Isla del Coco
Bahía de Coronado
Golfo Dulce
PANAMA
National Parks:
1 Guanacaste
2 Santa Rosa
3 Tamarindo
4 Rincon de la Vieja
5 Palo Verde
6 Barra Honda
7 Arenal
8 Juan Castro Blanco
9 Volcán Poás
10 Braulio Carrillo
11 Volcán Irazú
12 M.N. Guayabo
13 Tapanti
14 Chirripo
15 Internacional la Amistad (section Costa Rica)
16 Manuel Antonio
17 Isla del Coco
18 Marino Ballena
19 Corcovado
20 Cahuita
21 Tortuguero
Principal Indian reservations:
22 Ujarras-Salitre-Cabagra
23 Osa
24 Cocles/ Këköldi (Bribri, Cabérares)
25 Tayni
26 Telyre
27 Chirripo
28 Talamanca (Guaymi)
29 Matambú (Chorotegas)

in establishing the Central American Alianza de Desarollo Sostenible (Alliance for Sustainable Development), a cooperative strategy emphasizing environmentalism as a key to democratization and poverty reduction. In the context of this new collaboration, Central American states have held joint discussions on topics such as sustainable production, bio-diversity, energy, urban planning, and environmental education. In the course of the 1990s Costa Rica has concluded a bilateral agreement with the United States to tackle the causes of the greenhouse effect and has signed treaties with European countries on sustainable development.

Costa Rica has also led the way in other innovative environmental initiatives. In 1997, for instance, it signed a "carbon bond" deal with Norway, in a much-publicized gesture aimed at reducing carbon emissions and the "greenhouse effect" in the world's atmosphere. Under the agreement, the Norwegian government bought 200,000 tons worth of carbon bonds, in effect paying Costa Rica to preserve its forests and plant new trees as a means of neutralizing atmospheric emissions. Based on the idea that forests absorb carbon dioxide and release oxygen into the atmosphere, the agreement recognizes the role of a country like Costa Rica in improving not only its own environment, but that of the world. The deal has allowed the government to begin reforestation and forest conservation projects in a 50-square-mile area and to develop emission-saving hydro-electric plants.

The Supreme Court of Justice supports the government's environmental policy, stating in an important judgment that where the protection of the environment is concerned the interests of the state take precedence over the interests of private initiative. The Court was rejecting the application of a private foundation which wanted to use parrots living in the wild for breeding programs.

Environmental organizations and growing numbers of Costa Ricans keep a critical eye on the government's policy with respect to the environment, many pointing out that its conservation strategy is largely incompatible with its drive to increase agro-exports. The carbon bond initiative has also come in for criticism, since opponents argue that it implicitly allows richer countries to carry on polluting, while poorer ones are expected to clean up the atmosphere on their behalf. But environmentalism has become a popular concept among large sectors of the population, especially rural communities which have benefited from integration into conservation schemes. Many people who in the past were still felling wood illegally are now championing the cause of forest conservation and are, for example, being trained to be nature guides. In some cases, however, independent environmental organizations have come into direct conflict with the government.

Tropical hardwood is still cut in Costa Rica.
Replanting, however, takes place on a large scale.

B&U Int.Picture Service/3F Prod.

Stone Container Corporation

At the beginning of 1995 the environment movement secured a victory in a controversial legal case. After intensive protests from Costa Rican environment organizations and Greenpeace, the U.S. paper-making concern Stone Container Corporation was forced to retreat to an alternative location near Golfito to build its wood-processing factory and attached docks. The original site location in Punta Estrella on the Golfo Dulce would have entailed extensive damage to the environment, and activists feared that the project would interrupt the "natural biological corridor" between the Corcovado National Park and the Peñas Blancas Game Reservation (on the Panamanian border). Significantly, the governments of both Calderón and Figueres insisted that the project was in keeping with "sustainable development," but Figueres eventually gave in to the protests.

Canal Seco

Another project has been a controversial topic of discussion for some 25 years in Costa Rica but is unlikely ever to come to fruition. The *Canal Seco* or "dry canal" is the name given to a projected land connection between the Pacific (Puerto Soley near La Cruz in Guanacaste) and the Caribbean (Parismina near Dorotea in Limón). Ships which are too large for the Panama Canal would have to load their containers onto electric express trains which would transport them from one coast to the other.

Those in favor of the initiative say that the dry canal (costing an estimated $1.5 billion) would compete efficiently with the Panama Canal and that the project would have a positive impact on Costa Rica's economy. The planners, meanwhile, promise 50,000 new jobs at least. Opponents point out that the vast scale of the project would inevitably have a devastating effect on the environment. It is interesting to note that similar plans exist in Nicaragua, Mexico, and Panama itself.

Tourism

Keen monkey-watchers are recommended to go to the Manuel Antonio National Park on the Pacific, one of the last refuges of the rare *mono titi* or squirrel monkey. Within this small 1,700-acre park live no fewer than 350 different varieties of birds, as well as lizards, peccaries, snakes, iguanas, small bears, and many other animals. Manuel Antonio is the most popular of the national parks, which is not surprising in view of its splendid beaches, amazing views, coral reefs, and unusual rock formations. Indeed, so many visitors have come here that the very survival of its flora and fauna has been jeopardized. Animals have retreated from view or changed in behavior, while entreaties not to feed the monkeys are widely ignored. Entry to the park has therefore been restricted to a maximum of 800 visitors a day and in 1994 the entrance fees were also raised by more than 1,000 per cent. Foreign tourists had to pay $15 a day each, but Costa Ricans were allowed in for less.

Tourists and tourist organizations reacted angrily, demanding alternative measures or a national pass system with a single price for entry to all national parks. The minister for tourism, René Castro, defended the price rises, explaining that the increased revenue was necessary for the conservation of nature areas. "If two of you go to the cinema in the United States it will cost you $12. For a little more you can see everything here, live and all in full color."

In the aftermath of the price hike, the National Chamber of Tourism registered a dramatic fall in the number of visitors to the national parks, even among Costa Ricans. Castro at first doubted the figures but then changed tack, introducing a multi-entry "green pass" which has made visiting the national parks much cheaper again.

Treasure Island

Over the course of time more than 500 expeditions have been undertaken to the Isla del Coco, Coconut Island, to find a legendary pirate treasure. On one of the largest uninhabited islands of the world, 400 miles away from the Costa Rican coast in the Pacific, treasure worth hundreds of millions of dollars, once the booty of Spanish privateers, is reputed to be buried.

More verifiable are the 200 waterfalls, rainforests, exceptional varieties of flora and fauna, tropical fish and sharks off the coast. "Treasure Island" was designated a national park in 1987, but park-keepers have only been active over the last four years. There is no money available for proper maintenance, and the park-keepers are barely able to tackle the illegal fishing which takes place around the island.

René Castro, the tourism minister, has enlisted the support of the Frenchman Jean-Michel Cousteau, son of the late underwater film-maker and environmental activist, Jacques Cousteau, to develop a plan for the environmental conservation of the island. He fears that the fishing fleets which have been banished from the coast of the Ecuadorean Galápagos Islands will start hunting off the coast of the Isla del Coco.

Mass Tourism or Eco-Tourism?

Environmental organizations fear that tourism on a grand scale will prove disastrous for the environment. They blame the Calderón government for the systematic exploitation of coastal areas, where hotels with hundreds of rooms have sprung up. An alliance of environmental organizations awarded Calderón's tourism minister the "devil's prize for ecology" for what they called his "hypocritical eco-tourism." Many Ticos can no longer afford a vacation in their own country, because hotel prices are too high and large swathes of the coast have been effectively privatized. As Costa Rica aims for "up-market" tourists, it effectively discourages many of its own citizens from enjoying its attractions.

Under pressure from the environmental movement, a few huge projects have been scrapped or postponed in recent years, but plans for other controversial large-scale tourist centers are still under consideration. The government invariably argues that mega-projects carry the prospect of employment and foreign investment (although any jobs created are usually temporary work).

The much-cited alternative is what is known as eco-tourism, in which the tourist is supposed to contribute to the protection of the environment by following approved and culturally sensitive guidelines. These include avoiding unnecessary intrusion into wildlife habitats, remaining aware of the needs of local communities, and supporting sustainable and small-scale local initiatives. Eco-tourism has become big business in Costa Rica and elsewhere, and some observers believe that in many cases it is little more than a public relations exercise, concealing old-fashioned, unsustainable practices.

In some cases, eco-tourism has contributed to environmental problems, exacerbating pressures on wildlife habitats. In the Caño Negro wildlife refuge, on the Río Frío near the Nicaraguan border, a swampy system of canals and lagoons contains an astonishing 400 bird species (more than in

Costa Rica as a tourist paradise. The Pacific coast. *B&U Int. Picture Service/3F Prod.*

the whole of Europe), as well as crocodiles, monkeys, sloths, and turtles. Yet despite protection of the area since 1984, human activity has caused widespread damage. Illegal cattle grazing takes place during the dry season, when waters recede by ten feet or more and rich grasses sprout. Deforestation is a problem, as is the presence of hunters in search of caymans and crocodiles. The presence of motor boats, transporting bird-watchers and other tourists, has added to these disturbances, scaring away some species and polluting areas of water.

Much worse is the damage inflicted by eco-tourism on the leatherback sea turtle, the world's largest reptile, which can be seen between October and March each year on the beach at La Baula national park in Guanacaste province. In the 1970s thousands of these turtles, some weighing over a ton, congregated on the Playa Grande beach to lay their eggs, attracting crowds of tourists. Some visitors took night-time photographs of the turtles, causing blindness in several cases; others attempted to ride on their backs, while groups of up to 150 tourists gathered around laying females. By the mid-1990s, the numbers of turtles arriving on the beach had fallen to a few hundred, prompting the government to establish unobtrusive viewing platforms and to provide an increase in national park rangers to deter poachers and tourists alike.

Papagayo

Guanacaste has, with some justification, been called the Hawaii of the nineties. What was until recently the virgin coastline of the province bordering on Nicaragua now already attracts many tourists, but over the next few years a massive new influx of visitors is expected. A new international airport is being built near the city of Liberia to relieve the pressure on San José. About twenty years ago the government initiated the so-called Papagayo project, which provides for the leasing of 10,000 acres of state-owned land to tourist developers along the 35-mile coastline of the Bahía de Culebra. Construction is already underway, and some 15,000 new hotel rooms are planned in the first stage. The project's architect is even predicting the building of a total of 60,000 rooms over the next twenty years. In 1995, the total capacity in Costa Rica was 15,000 hotel rooms.

Papagayo, taking its name from the Bay of Papagayo, is the biggest single tourist project in Central America. The plan has attracted a great deal of criticism and, following all manner of judicial actions brought by the Costa Rican ombudsman and by the national and international environmental movements, has been constantly adapted. A Mexican firm, Situr, has come under particular fire, especially since opponents believe that the Costa Rican government has been suspiciously over-generous in its dealings with the company. Citing unregulated tree-felling, mangrove clearance, and dredging, critics fear for the huge amount of damage that Papagayo will cause to the environment and to archaeological sites related to the Chorotega culture. Irregularities are also said to have been committed in the plan's development, although a court in San José acquitted a former tourism minister and twelve former directors of the Costa Rican Institute of Tourism of charges of embezzlement and negligence. The first hotel opened its doors in 1995.

Green Bananas

In the 1970s and 1980s, Standard Fruit/Dole workers in Costa Rica and other banana-producing countries were exposed to large doses of the pesticide DBCP. After it had come to light in the United States that workers who had been in contact with DBCP had been affected with permanent infertility and with stomach and skin cancer, the toxic material was prohibited in the 1970s. But some banana companies in Costa Rica continued regardless to use the pesticide for many years afterwards, and when Costa Rica eventually banned DBCP in 1987, Standard Fruit used what remained on plantations in Honduras. For a small number of those workers affected in Costa Rica compensation has been paid, varying from $7,500 to $9,000, a sum which critics dismissed as merely a means of buying them off. Further thousands are still awaiting compensation from the multinationals, frustrated and disillusioned by the slow pace of litigation. More than 10,000 Costa Rican workers are currently represented in legal cases in the U.S., yet with little prospect of imminent compensation. Mostly poor and landless rural workers, they are suffering from cancer, impotence, and sterility caused by the chemicals. The Second International Water Tribunal in Amsterdam also condemned Standard Fruit in 1992 for serious pollution of the Atlantic region of Costa Rica, the consequence of banana cultivation in the Valle de la Estrella.

Within the banana industry, which uses a great number of toxic and pollutant substances, efforts are slowly being made to operate in a more environmentally friendly manner. The Costa Rican environmental group Fundación Ambio and the U.S.-based Rainforest Alliance have now issued an "eco" seal of approval to banana growers who observe various environmental guidelines in their production. The seal of approval has been determined in collaboration with scientists, environmental activists, and banana growers. Although certainly not all banana farmers and plantation owners are interested in the project, there are some growers who are keen on acquiring the seal of approval. There are, for instance, already two plantations belonging to the U.S. Chiquita Brands company which have the ECO-OK seal, and Chiquita wants to obtain the "green seal" for all twelve of its plantations.

The banana farmers who want to be given the seal of approval have to make a contribution to the reforestation of the areas which border on their plantations. They have to discontinue using the most dangerous of the pesticides and have to train their workers how to handle toxic chemicals. They also have to give priority to the recycling of plastic and organic waste.

A factory recently opened in Costa Rica which manufactures a special sort of paper from banana leaves and stalks, and the new business is hoping in the future to make boxes for banana and coffee packing from organic waste. The manufacturer gets his waste material from the banana plantations in the Atlantic region, waste that otherwise would probably disappear into the rivers or sea or would be burned. The reactions of the big banana companies to this new project are cautious. As its manager explained to the English-language weekly *Costa Rica Today*, "They think that the project is fantastic, as long as I can actually do it!"

5 CULTURE: THE AMERICAN WAY

Argentina has tango; Peru, Mexico, Guatemala, and Bolivia have their Indian cultures; Colombia has salsa and Gabriel García Márquez, the Nobel Prize winner for literature. So what can Costa Rica offer in terms of culture? The answer is not simple. Although the country is part of Latin America, both geographically and culturally, it has a less defined character of its own compared with the other countries of the continent. Folk-art, folklore, and local cultural forms are much less a part of everyday life than elsewhere in the region. An important factor in this absence of national culture is the relative smallness of the country's indigenous population and the overwhelming dominance of European migration in the nineteenth century.

Ticos identify with the United States much more than with other countries in the region, which they tend to regard as "underdeveloped." The U.S. is the undisputed role model, culturally and economically; McDonalds, Pizza Hut, and CNN are an indispensable part of most people's lives, and the majority of Costa Ricans aspire to the consumerist lifestyle of the USA rather than that of their poorer neighbors.

Such American influence is by no means surprising; the U.S. is by far Costa Rica's most important trading partner and American television series are shown all day on national and satellite channels. Most tourists who visit Costa Rica are Americans, while of the 260,000 Costa Ricans who made foreign trips in 1994, 52 per cent went to the U.S. on business, to visit friends, or on shopping trips or to Disneyland.

Ticos

Costa Ricans refer to themselves as Ticos, a nickname also applied to them by Latin Americans all over the continent. Affectionate rather then pejorative, the word, Tico is said to stem from the old colonial saying: "*somos todos hermaniticos*" ("we are all little brothers"). The nickname also reflects the Costa Rican custom of adding the diminutive "tico" to all manner of words. While other Spanish-speaking countries use a diminutive in the form of "-ito," Costa Ricans often combine the two in a sort of super-diminutive. Something small is therefore not simply *chico* or *chiqito*, but *chiquitico*. Further diminutives can be added to make the thing in question extra tiny or *chiqui-ti-ti-tico*.

"*Tiquismos*" are expressions peculiar to Costa Rican language and culture. A kitten, for instance, is a *gatito* anywhere else in Spanish, but a *gatico* in Costa Rica. "*Un momentito*" (just a moment) becomes "*un momentico*," while at a garage you might have your *aceitico* (literally, little oil) checked. These linguistic peculiarities reinforce a Costa Rican self-image and value system, in which a favorite national dish like *gallo pinto* (rice and beans) is simply "*muy tico*" or very Costa Rican.

Regional Differences

Distinct from mainstream Costa Rican suburbia, the province of Guanacaste, bordering on Nicaragua, does have its own distinctive culture. *Guanacasteños* have an accent which has much in common with the Spanish spoken in Nicaragua, and people clip the letter "s" as do they do in the neighboring country. During the Spanish era Guanacaste was governed and colonized from Managua. In 1824, during the era of the Central American Federation, Guanacaste sought agreement to become part of Costa Rica and although the Federation granted the request, the region remained a bone of contention between Nicaragua and Costa Rica for a long time afterwards.

Music, folklore, customs, personal characteristics, and the landscape itself differ considerably from the rest of Costa Rica. Most of the province is in fact one extensive plain, with Santa Rosa, Costa Rica's oldest national park, situated in the northwest. With cattle-ranching the main economic activity, Guanacaste has lost most of its tropical dry forest and has developed a *sabanero* (cowboy) culture of rodeos and machismo. Liberia, its capital, has been nicknamed the "White City" and is unique in Costa Rica on account of its unspoiled colonial architecture and atmosphere. Some houses have two front-doors, *puertas del sol*, the door on the eastern side letting in the morning sun and the door on the southern side allowing heat to escape in the late afternoon. In Liberia's Museo del Sabanero (Cowboy Museum) the past and present of the region's cattle-drivers live on. Pots, lassoes, agricultural implements, machetes, axes, saddles: all the paraphernalia of ranching life are on display.

The Costa Rican writer Héctor Zúñiga honored his province in his sentimental poem of rural life, *Guanacaste:*

La brisa me acaricia en la corral,
la brisa mañanera,
va levantando el sol por el maizal
y alumbra la pradera.

The breeze caresses me in the yard,
the morning breeze,
the sun comes rising through
the cornfield
and lights up the meadow.

En la grama el rocío se ve platear
por entre la tranquera
potrillos que jugando al retozar
alegran el lugar.

The morning dew covers the
grass with silver
and inside the paddock
young foals frisk
playfully, animating the farm
lands.

Viene ya el arreador,
ya se le oye silbar,

Here comes the foreman now,
you can hear him whistling.

Guanacastan scene in Liberia. The door at the corner is a *puerta del sol.*

Tjabel Daling

pasa el enrejador, porque van a ordeñar. Sabaneros que van al zaguán a ensillar, ocinera que canta al palmear.	He goes inside the enclosure because it is time for milking. Cowboys saddle the horses, the kitchen maid sings and claps her hands in time.
Guanacaste yo viví con tu lucha, cielo y mar y aunque esté lejos de ti nunca te podré olvidar	Guanacaste, I lived with your struggle, your sky and sea and though I am far away from you, I will never forget you.

Mariachis

La Esmerelda cafe is the headquarters of San José's League of Mariachis, its own version of Mexico's troubadours. Dozens of Mexican-style Mariachis, dressed in sombreros and sequined costumes, wait in front of the entrance or hang around in the café itself, while a notice in the hallway shows which band is playing that evening. Originally from Mexico but now adapted to Costa Rican tastes, San José's Mariachis perform throughout the night, serenading customers at other venues such as the Soda Palace in the center of San José, open twenty-four hours a day. Their audiences have to pay handsomely, of course, tourists paying more than Ticos.

Folk Festivals

Almost every town and every village celebrates once a year the festival of its patron saint's day, the *fiesta patronal.* At first glance, these events do not differ too much from any other fair or festival, with their emphasis on eating, drinking, music, and merrymaking. But in Costa Rica no festival is complete without bull fights (*corridas*), which in true Costa Rican tradition, are quite different from those of Spain. In keeping with their much-vaunted pacifism, Ticos are proud that their bulls are not killed during the bull fights, which are meant to be demonstrations of *sabanero* prowess.

The *torero* or bullfighter goads the animal, challenges it, and pursues it until it is tired. Cowboys on horseback then lasso the bull and lead it away. Bulls are sometimes ridden, or spectators are allowed to enter the ring and challenge the bulls. The bull usually comes off well from such encounters, but this by no means always applies to the bullfighter. Towards the end of 1994 during five days of folk festivals in the village of Zapote, the Red Cross had to deal with 193 injuries, and seventeen inexperienced *toreros* were taken to hospital.

Carnaval Limón

The black population in the province of Limón, the majority of whom are Protestants, is small, and the few tens of thousands of descendants of former immigrants from Jamaica account for only two per cent of Costa Rica's population and fourteen per cent of the province's people. Afro-Costa Ricans speak Patua, a dialect of English, among themselves or American English, while the younger generation also speaks Spanish.

The climax of the year in the run-down port of Puerto Limón is the carnival on October 12 in celebration of Columbus's arrival in the Americas. For three or four days on end *Limonenses* dance the calypso, and theater, music, fireworks, special activities for children, street parades, horse races, and Tico-style bullfights all make the Limón Carnival the best festival in Costa Rica.

The Jamaican immigrants originally had their own festivals and sports but gradually, to the regret of many older people, certain of these traditions have become lost. "Slavery Day" was celebrated up until the 1960s, in commemoration of the day that Britain abolished slavery in its colonies. An inhabitant of Limón recalled it in the 1970s:

> All the Jamaicans celebrated the day with a great deal of eating and drinking. We slaughtered a pig and a cow. There were horse races, we played cricket. It was a splendid festival. But now it has all been swept away. Only older people still keep the tradition. Younger people are no longer bothered.

Cricket too has disappeared, even though in the province of Limón the sport was incredibly popular in the 1920s and 1930s, when the United Fruit Company sponsored various teams to compete in a provincial competition. After the games there was often a public picnic, with the women preparing a Creole meal of rice and beans and Caribbean music enjoyed well into the night.

The outbreak of the Second World War dealt Costa Rican cricket its death blow. All cricket equipment had to come from England and during the war supplies dried up. Cricket was superseded by baseball and later on by soccer.

Literature

Many Costa Rican authors concentrate on contemporary social issues or work current themes into historical novels. After a long tradition of literary nationalism, a group of writers emerged around 1940 who placed far greater emphasis on social themes and "committed literature." This "generation of 1940" was headed by Carlos Salazar Herrera (1906-1980), Carlos Luís Fallas (1906-1966), Joaquín Gutiérrez (1918-), and Fabián Dobles (1918-), all of whom were Communist Party activists or closely associated with its political aims. Many writers today are still inspired by the social realism of the "generation of 1940."

The most important of these writers was Fallas, who started as a worker on a banana plantation, worked his way up to become a trade union leader and was co-founder of the Communist Party and joint organizer of the great banana strike in 1934. He wrote one of the great classics of Costa Rican literature, which is still required reading in the country's schools. *Mamita Yunai* (1941) describes the terrible conditions and poverty on the banana plantations of the United Fruit Company. Gutiérrez's work portrays the lives of the black population of the Atlantic coastal region, a context in which Quince Duncan (1940-) is also an important name. He has written novels, short stories, and essays about life in Limón, the role of blacks in Costa Rican literature, and the problems of racism.

In recent years a number of outstanding books have appeared which deal with specifically Costa Rican historical themes. Alberto Camas recreates in *Los molinos del Dios* (The Mills of God) the golden age of the coffee planters who often came from Germany. Tatiana Lobo Wiehoff takes as her central theme in *Asalto al paraíso* (Assault on Paradise) the Indian uprising against the Spanish in the Talamanca mountains. More topically, the negative impact of tourism on the Caribbean community is explored in the "ecological" novel, *La loca de Gandoca* (The Mad Woman of Gandoca) by Anacristina Rossi.

Women have always made a significant contribution to Costa Rican literature. One of the country's best-known writers is María Isabel Carvajal (1888-1949), who wrote under the pen-name of Carmen Lyra. She produced novels in the social realism genre, but was most popular as a writer of children's books. Young feminist writers have in the last few years achieved a particularly high profile. The poet, actress, and playwright Ana Istarú is in the eyes of many the "feminist voice" of Costa Rica, attacking machismo in her poetry. Istarú has already won international prizes with her poetry.

In the Costa Rican bullfight the bull stays alive *B&U Int. Picture Service/3F Prod.*

The following poem is a fragment from her collection *a Estacicón de Fiebre*:

El novio se contenta
al padre alienta
que en América Central
siempre se encuentra
u hija virgen asexual
como el varón domeña
y preña
en América Central
y panameña
y de este fálica
omnipotencia
mi rebelión obreras
me defienda

The bridegroom is satisfied
Father heaves a sigh of relief
because in Central America
his daughter always enters
as a virgin and asexual
into marriage.
This unwritten law
shows how the man
compels the woman to obedience
and sexually subjugates her.
In my work I rebel
and as a woman I defend myself
against this omnipotent
phallic power.

Unfortunately, the literary climate in Costa Rica leaves much to be desired, and most Ticos are not enthusiastic readers. Literature and poetry are published in small print-runs, and a book which sells 5,000 copies is a notable exception. Despite the country's high level of literacy, there are few good bookstores and publishers. In many cases, local writers have to take second place to the big names of Latin American and Spanish literature as well as translated authors from the U.S.

Soccer

Even before they can walk, boast Costa Ricans, Ticos and Ticas can play soccer, a sport which is a national obsession, even among women. Every village has its own soccer pitch, there is a strong professional league, and in recent years the national team has notched up reasonably good results. In 1990 Costa Rica succeeded in qualifying for the World Cup finals in Italy, eventually reaching the last sixteen and beating Scotland in the process. Ex-President Arías attended all the matches and on one occasion accused the referee of attempting to fix the result. Arias later apologized with the observation that it is a fundamental human right to be a soccer fan.

The importance of soccer to Costa Rican life is demonstrated each year at the climax to the national competition, which normally features a fiercely partisan encounter between the country's two best teams, Alajuelense (from Alajuela) and the capital's Saprissa. Soccer's less desirable dimensions are also familiar to Costa Ricans. During the final of the national competition in 1993 supporters of the finalists, Cartago and Heredia, came to blows, breaking through the perimeter fences and invading the pitch of the Cartago stadium. The national guard had to intervene to separate the two sides fighting each other and the match was abandoned in chaos. The Cartago team later brought a legal action before the Supreme Court for "violation of its human rights," while the match had to be replayed in an empty stadium. Heredia won the replay. Costa Ricans were also traumatized in October 1996 when over a hundred people were killed in the disaster at the overcrowded Mateo Flores soccer stadium in Guatemala City, shortly before Guatemala's match with Costa Rica.

Costa Rican soccer received a boost in 1997, when the 19-year-old Alajuelense star, Froylan Ledezma, signed a $5-million contract with the Dutch team Ajax. Four other Costa Ricans currently play in European leagues, including Derby County's Paulo César Wanchope, and it is thought that much more sporting talent remains undiscovered in Costa Rica.

Despite such successes, the world of soccer in Costa Rica is mostly a murky blend of conflict and scandal: fraud and constant jockeying for power within the national soccer league; disunity between the league and the soccer teams; drug-taking players who threaten to go on strike because the soccer season is too long and because they have to play too many matches. In the national league alone clubs have to play 56 matches. Soccer players are now coming out strongly in favor of their own trade union and a collective labor agreement to regulate their conditions of work.

WHERE TO GO, WHAT TO SEE

Although Costa Rica is a small country compared to other, rival Latin American tourist destinations, it has a vast amount to offer in terms of landscapes, flora and fauna, and activities. Energetic visitors can go horse-riding, trekking, and, of course, can walk in the country's 35 national parks. There are trips to coffee *fincas*, rodeos, and white water rapids. You can see jaguars, tapirs and the famed and elusive quetzal bird, symbol of Guatemala. Above all, it is nature which overwhelms the visitors with its sheer variety and splendor, embracing still-active volcanoes, cloudforest, and rampant tropical vegetation. And for those unmoved by Costa Rica's almost unparalleled natural attractions, there are always the beaches, including some of the best in the region.

Until recently, visitors arriving in Costa Rica had to fly into San José's airport. The opening of the Daniel Odúber Quirós International Airport (named after a 1970s president) near Liberia now means that tourists bound for the beaches and national parks of the northern Guanacaste province no longer have to pass through the capital.

But it would be a shame to miss San José altogether, even though many people tend to dismiss the city as lacking in character and culture. Regular earthquakes have demolished much of its colonial architecture, and concrete now tends to be the norm, but the climate is very pleasant and the surrounding scenery impressive. Once you have worked out the intricacies of the city's grid system (*avenidas* run east to west, *calles* north to south), it is fairly easy to find your way around, although driving in the narrow and more polluted streets of the center is not recommended.

Worth a visit is the National Theater, an ornate testimony to the country's debt to coffee, "the golden bean." Gold plate, red plush, and marble abound, creating an atmosphere of rather faded splendor. Fittingly, there is a good coffee bar. Next-door on the same square, the Plaza de la Cultura, is the Gold Museum, with a fine collection of pre-Columbian artifacts. The National Museum (Calle 17, Avenida Central & 2) has a fascinating mix of archaeology, natural history, and anthropology, with an emphasis on Costa Rica's indigenous past and the violence stemming from colonization. In contrast, ex-President Arias' Nobel Peace prize is on display, reflecting the country's more pacific modern self-image. The Jade Musum, on the eleventh floor of the INS building (Avenida 7, Calles 9-11), houses the largest collection of jade in the Americas and is beautifully laid out. The view over the city and the surrounding mountains is also spectacular.

There are plenty of bars, restaurants, and discos in San José, but few are really distinctive, except perhaps for La Esmeralda (Avenida 2, Calle

7), the city's Mariachi center. El Pueblo commercial center has a number of decent bars and restaurants.

The capital's National Park has a patriotic monument, commemorating Costa Rica's role in the downfall of the U.S. adventurer, William Walker. Also honored is drummer-boy and national hero, Juan Santamaría, who is the main attraction at the museum at Alajuela, Costa Rica's second city and a cool midsummer resort. The museum, housed in a former jail, tells the story of Santamaría and the strange war against Walker's filibusters. Heredia and Cartago are the other two main towns in the Central Plateau. Earthquakes have demolished what might once have been interesting architecture, but Cartago's Basilica de Nuestra Señora de Los Angeles, rebuilt in 1926 in Byzantine style, is worth a visit, if only to see the offerings left by pilgrims to La Negrita, the country's patron saint, who reputedly cures all ills. She appeared first to a peasant girl in 1635, and since then pilgrimages have attracted thousands of faithful every year on August 2.

Some twenty miles north of Cartago is the Volcán Irazú, one of the country's main tourist attractions. A lunar landscape of gray ash, with a green algae-colored lake in the volcano's crater, the site offers great views from a height of more than 10,000 feet. You should go in the morning, since clouds and mist tend to spoil the view in the afternoon. Irazú has been dormant since March 1963, when it erupted during the state visit of U.S. President John F. Kennedy to Costa Rica.

Other volcanoes are more unpredictable, and the country sits in one of the world's most volatile geological areas. With nine out of Latin America's 42 active volcanoes and over 100 which are extinct, Costa Rica is built on unstable foundations. Fortunately, eruptions are rare, but one exception is the Volcán Arenal in the country's northwest which explodes every three to six hours and rumbles almost continuously. A big eruption in 1968 killed 78 people, and in 1988 a tourist was burnt to death by molten rock while hiking to the crater. But safe tours are organized from nearby Fortuna, including spectacular nocturnal sightings of orange lava flows. Close by are the spas of Tabacón, with hot sulfurous water, and a volcanic museum at La Vaca Muca. South of Arenal is Monteverde, where a two-and-a-half-hour journey up poor roads takes you to a Cloudforest Reserve, home to 400 bird species, including the quetzal. The settlement itself was founded in the 1950s by American Quakers and is an increasingly popular tourist destination, offering a range of accommodation, crafts, and locally-made produce.

Another active volcano, although less so than Arenal, is Rincón de la Vieja, about twenty miles northeast of Liberia. Bubbling lakes and pungent steam testify to the area's geological instability, while in the surrounding national park there are some 30 rivers and countless bird species. Nearby Santa Rosa National Park, established in 1971, has one of the country's richest arrays of natural diversity, encompassing mangroves, savanna, oak forests, and grasslands. The park is home to 115 species of mammals, including 50 species of bat, as well as 250 bird species. Within its boundaries is La Casona, the fortified farm house from which the plucky Santamaría is said to have dislodged William Walker's troops (although another version claims the site to be in Nicaragua).

Half of the Caribbean coast is protected territory, made up of national parks and wildlife refuges. Limón province covers the entire coastline from Nicaragua down to Panama, and is sparsely populated and underdeveloped. Limón is famous for its black population, but to the south are the indigenous Bribrí and Cabécar communities in the Talamanca region. At Puerto Viejo the Talamancan Eco-Tourism and Conservation Association (ATEC) promotes socially responsible tourism by providing information on both black and indigenous culture and by training local people as guides.

The town of Puerto Limón is run down and decaying, smashed by an earthquake in 1991. The travel writer and novelist Paul Theroux thought it "a steaming, stinking town of mud puddles and buildings discolored by dampness," asking, "Was there a dingier backwater in all the world?" Not all travelers will agree with this gloomy view, and the town comes into its own every October 12, when carnival takes over with its English Caribbean mix of cricket, calypso and reggae. Cahuita, down the coast towards Panama, has developed into an informal beach holiday center, although there are now drug-related problems and occasional robberies.

On the other, Pacific, coast, Quepos and the Manuel Antonio National Park have much better beaches, with excellent opportunities for snorkeling. Beware of rip tides, however, and steeply sloping beaches. Manuel Antonio was until recently a victim of its own success, and so many visitors were converging on the area that access had to be limited. Dominical, 25 miles south-east of Quepos, is also renowned for its beaches; one of the best is Playa Matapalo, recommended for surfing. Further north, Guanacaste has its share of good beaches, although the impact of mass tourism is most evident here. Liberia, a small cattle town with well-preserved white buildings, is worth a visit, even if the Cowboy Museum is something of a disappointment. The Nicoya peninsula is also feeling the effects of tourism, as large hotels take over some of the best beaches and coves. Playa del Coco, Playa Tamarindo, Playa Nosara, and Playa Sámara are all popular, Sámara in particular for its reputation as a safe swimming beach.

The remoteness of the Osa peninsula kept tourism at bay for many years, but this is now beginning to change. The region is rich in gold, and although prospectors were cleared from the Corcovado National Park in the mid-1980s, there is still a problem with illicit mining. Some ex-*oreros* have found work in eco-tourism projects, based around the town of Puerto Jiménez.

TIPS FOR TRAVELERS

Safety

Costa Rica is still a relatively safe country, but crime is on the rise. Although by North American and European standards, crime is not yet a major problem, Costa Ricans complain that the security situation has deteriorated, largely due to economic problems. Today's San José is not much safer than other big cities in Central America, and *pandillas* (youth gangs) operate in certain areas, including the center. A few spectacular kidnappings and robberies in tourist centers have caused panic, but travelers should beware of exaggeration. If a few basic precautions are followed, visitors are unlikely to face problems. Pickpockets mostly operate around bus stations, on buses, or in crowded markets. Don't carry expensive items in these situations or on beaches. Apart from San José itself, areas in which you should be extra careful are Limón (especially during carnival), Quepos, and the region around the Nicaraguan border.

Health

Some diseases such as malaria, cholera, and dengue have turned up again in recent years, after it was thought that they had been eradicated. Malaria and cholera are not a real threat in most of the country, and only travelers to the more remote areas of Talamanaca and Limón should be aware of the risks. Avoid raw fruit and salads, unless carefully washed and peeled; make sure that food is just cooked and, preferably, from hygienic premises. Tap water is safe to drink in San José, but it is probably wise to buy bottled water elsewhere. Mosquitoes can be a terrible nuisance, but mosquito repellents are widely available. On the beach, beware of sand flies and, more seriously, strong currents and undertow. Ask the locals whether it is safe to swim. One tourist ignored such advice recently and was reportedly eaten by crocodiles …

Women Travelers

Machismo is prevalent in Costa Rica, and single women can expect flirtatious remarks and hissing from passing men. Violent behavior is rare, but irritating gestures are commonplace. Do your best to ignore them. Most Ticos are kind and hospitable to all travelers.

Changing Money

You can change money at San José's airport until 5 pm. Most banks open from 9 am until 3 pm, although some branches stay open until later. Banks are busiest on Mondays and Fridays. You can change dollars at the bigger hotels in San José, but give the street moneychangers a wide berth, since they sometimes deal in counterfeit notes. A reliable address in central San José for changing dollars is the Pension Americana, Calle 2, Avenidas Central & 2. Most businesses accept Visa, MasterCard and American Express. The Costa Rican unit of currency is the *colón,* which fluctuates in relation to the dollar. Check rates.

Souvenirs

There is no shortage of souvenir shops in Costa Rica. T-shirts, jewelry, coffee beans, leather, and wood crafts are available in hundreds of shops in the capital. For wooden goods and furniture go to the village of Sarchí, about an hour northwest of San José; a good area for leather crafts is the suburb of Moravia. The Tienda de la Naturaleza at Volcán Poás national park, 35 miles from San José, sells handicrafts made by local rural communities, while cooperatives in Monteverde sell all kinds of interesting things, including excellent cheese. In San José, try the Mercado Nacional de Artesanía (Calle 11, Avenida 2 bis), the Mercado Central, and La Casona (Calle Central, Avenidas Central/1). Local artisans sell earrings, imported Guatemalan textiles, and pottery at the Plaza de la Cultura, mostly at weekends.

Children

There is no reason not to bring children to Costa Rica, since most *Ticos* are friendly towards them. San José has a very interesting children's museum, which is fun for adults as well. It is located in a former prison which looks like a castle at the north end of Calle 4. The Parque Nacional de Diversiones in La Uruca, west of San José, is an amusement park with many different rides.

Drugs

Costa Rica is a transshipment point for narcotics en route to the U.S., and it is not difficult to buy drugs in San José. Both buying and using are inadvisable, since penalties are very harsh.

ADDRESSES AND CONTACTS

Embassy of Costa Rica
2114 S Street NW
Washington, DC 20008
Tel: (202) 234-2945
Website: costarica-embassy.org

Embassy of Costa Rica
14 Lancaster Gate
London W2 3LH
Tel: (020) 7562-2855
Website: www.embcrlon.demon.co.uk

Global Exchange
2017 Mission Street #303
San Francisco, CA 94110
Tel: (415) 255-7296
Website: www.globalexchange.org
(educational tours including Central America)

Journey Latin America
12 & 13 Heathfield Terrace, Chiswick
London W4 4JE
Tel: (0208) 747-8315
Website: www.journeylatinamerica.co.uk
(specialist travel agents)

Costa Rica Expeditions
Calle Central, Avenida 3
San José
Tel: 257-0766
Website: www.costaricaexpeditions.com
(recommended local tour operator)

FURTHER READING AND BOOKSTORES

Bell, J., *Crisis in Costa Rica: The 1948 Revolution*, Austin, 1971.
Biesanz, R. et al., *The Costa Ricans*, New Jersey, 1982.
Dunkerley, J., *Power in the Isthmus: A Political History of Modern Central America*, London and New York, 1988.
Edelman, M. and J. Kenen (eds.), *The Costa Rica Reader*, New York, 1989.
Honey, M., *Hostile Acts: U.S. Policy in Costa Rica in the 1980s*, Gainesville, FL, 1994.
Krehm, W., *Democracies and Tyrannies of the Caribbean*, Westport, CT, 1984.
Lara, S., *Inside Costa Rica*, Albuquerque, 1995.
McNeil, J., *Costa Rica: The Rough Guide*, London and New York, 1996.
Seligson, M., *Peasants of Costa Rica and the Development of Agrarian Capitalism*, Wisconsin, 1980.
Trejos, A., *Illustrated Geography of Costa Rica*, San José, 1991.

Fiction and Poetry

Dobles, F., *Years Like Brief Days*, London, and Chester Springs, PA, 1996.
Fallas, C.L., *Mamita Yunai*, San José, 1941.
Hopkinson, A. (ed.), *Lovers and Comrades: Women's Resistance Poetry from Central America*, London, 1989. Poems by Ana Istarú, Janina Fernández, and Lilly Guardia, among others.
Naranjo, C., *There Never Was a Once Upon a Time*, Pittsburgh, PA, 1990.

Local Bookstores

The Bookshop,
Avenida 1, Calle 1/3, San José

Chispas,
Avenida 0/1, Calle 7, San José

Lehmann,
Avenida 0, Calle 1/3, San José

FACTS AND FIGURES

GEOGRAPHY

Official name: República de Costa Rica.
Situation: between 8° 02' and 11° 58' N and 82° 30' and 85° 58' W; distance north-south along Pacific coast: 287 miles; distance between Cabo and Santa Elena-Colorado: 160 miles.
Surface area: 19,725 square miles, including some islands such as Isla de Chira (17 square miles) in the Bay of Nicoya and the Isla de Coco in the Pacific (8 square miles).
Administrative division: 7 *provincias* (1994, population x 1000): San José (1183), Alajuela (562), Cartago (375), Puntarenas (344), Heredia (296), Limón (253), Guanacaste (216); the provinces are subdivided into 81 *cantones* (cantons) and 434 *distritos* (districts).
Capital: San José (2000: 1.2 million inhabitants); 49% of the population live in the San José conurbation.
Other large towns (2000, population x 1,000): Alajuela (250), Cartago (150), Limón (150), Puntarenas (300).
Infrastructure: road network (2000): 23,161 miles, about 4,000 miles of which are national highways; railway network: San José is linked by rail with Puerto Limón on the Caribbean coast (since 1990 partly out of use owing to earthquakes) and Puerto Caldera and Puntarenas on the Pacific, also railway lines for banana transport, total (2000): 590 miles; Juan Santamaría International Airport near San José, international airport being built near Liberia; largest sea ports: Caldera, Puntarenas, Limón/Moín, Golfito; smaller ports: Quepos, Colorado, and Cahuita.
Relief and landscape: the most important feature in the landscape is the mountain range which bisects the country from northwest to southeast. This is formed by the Cordillera de Guanacaste, a series of mostly extinct volcanoes, the highest being the Volcán Santa María at 5,927 feet; then, to the south of the natural lake of Arenal, the Cordillera de Tilarán, likewise of volcanic origin, with the active Volcán Arenal (5,356 feet) to one side; then the Cordillera Central with seven active volcanoes, the highest being Volcán Irazú at 11,257 feet, and in the south the Cordillera de Talamanca with the Cerro Chirripó (12,526 feet), the country's highest peak. The last ranges enclose the central plateau, the Valle or Meseta Central; this extends to 31 by 15.5 miles (about 1,545 square miles, 8% of Costa Rica), lying at an average altitude of 3,300 feet (San José 3,772 feet); two-thirds of the population live in this small area. The area surrounding the Meseta Central is marked by volcanoes such as the Roás, Barva, Irazú, and Turrialba. In the south the Fila Costeña (the coastal range) runs parallel to the Talamanca range; between the two mountain ranges lies the Valle General. To the north of the mountain ranges a lowland plateau (*llanura*) extends beyond the landspits and the sandy shores of the Caribbean coast, crossed by numerous rivers, most of which flow into the Río San Juan; along the northern frontier the plateau runs almost as far as the Pacific coast. The coastal region along the Pacific is hilly, with occasional small coastal plains (the largest being the plain of the Río Tempisque); typical of the region are the many bays and peninsulas.
Climate and vegetation: because of its situation near the equator, temperature differences at sea level (*tierra caliente)* are negligible (Limón average 86° F,

Golfito average 84° F); the lowland plateaus up to 1,970 feet in the north and up to 2,300 feet in the south were formerly totally covered by tropical rainforest and mangrove forests (particularly to the north of Puerto Limón). Here one now finds large numbers of banana and cocoa plantations. In the plains along the Caribbean coast rain falls throughout the year (more than 120 inches, and up to amounts exceeding 230 inches near Colorado); along the Pacific coast there is an alternating wet and dry season; the vegetation in the northwest, in Guanacaste (40-80 inches), the region with the longest dry season (December to April), is dry savanna (now often grazing land). Between 2,000 feet and 5,400 feet is the temperate zone *(tierra templada)*, originally with oak trees, some losing their leaves in the dry season, but now densely populated and for the most part given over to cultivation; the Meseta Central lies in this zone and almost all the coffee is grown here. The average temperature in San José is 69° F and the annual rainfall lies between 60 and 80 inches. Above 5,410 feet there is a great deal of rainfall and there is frequently low-hanging cloud *(terra fria*, average temperature 53-60° F); the cloud forests lie on the mountain slopes. On the cold highest peaks of the mountain ranges *(tierra helada*, average temperature less than 53° F) there is *páramo*, the grassy vegetation which is also abundant in the High Andes of Peru and Bolivia.
Best tourist season: all year, the dry season (December-April) being slightly preferable.

POPULATION

Population (2000 est.): 3.71 million (1996: 3.34 million).
Annual population growth: 2000: 1.69%; 1990-1995: 2.3%; 1970-1980: 2.8%.
Population density (1996): 160 inhabitants per sq. mile.
Urbanization (1996): 49%.
Fertility (2000 est.): a Costa Rican woman has an average of 2.5 children.
Age structure (2000 est.): 0-14: 32%; 15-64: 63%; 65+: 5%.
Birth rate (2000 est.): 20.7 per 1,000 inhabitants.
Mortality rate (2000 est.): 4.3 per 1,000 inhabitants.
Infant mortality (2000 est.): 11.5 per 1,000 live births.
Average life expectancy (2000 est.): 76; women 78, men 73.
Health care (1985-93): population with access to health centers/safe drinking water (urban/rural): 100/63% and 100/86%; 1 doctor per 962 inhabitants (1996).
Literacy rate (1995 est.): 95%.
Education: the 1869 Constitution established the right to free education; 19% of the state budget is spent on education; compulsory schooling from 7 to 15; the average number of years of schooling is 5.7; all children attend primary school, 43% have secondary education, 28% follow higher education courses.
Universities: Six universities, including National University in San José and one "open university."
Social development index: (UNDP Human Development Index 1999): 45th position out of total 174 positions (U.S. 3rd, UK 10th); in 1990 the UN declared Costa Rica to be the developing country with the best Human Development Index.
Ethnic composition: whites (including mestizos) 94%, African origin 3%, Amerindian 1%, Chinese 1%, other 1%.
Religion: Roman Catholic (state religion) 85%; evangelical Protestant churches 14%.
Languages: Spanish (official); English (Limón region); Indian languages: Bribri, Cabecar, Guaymi, Maleko.

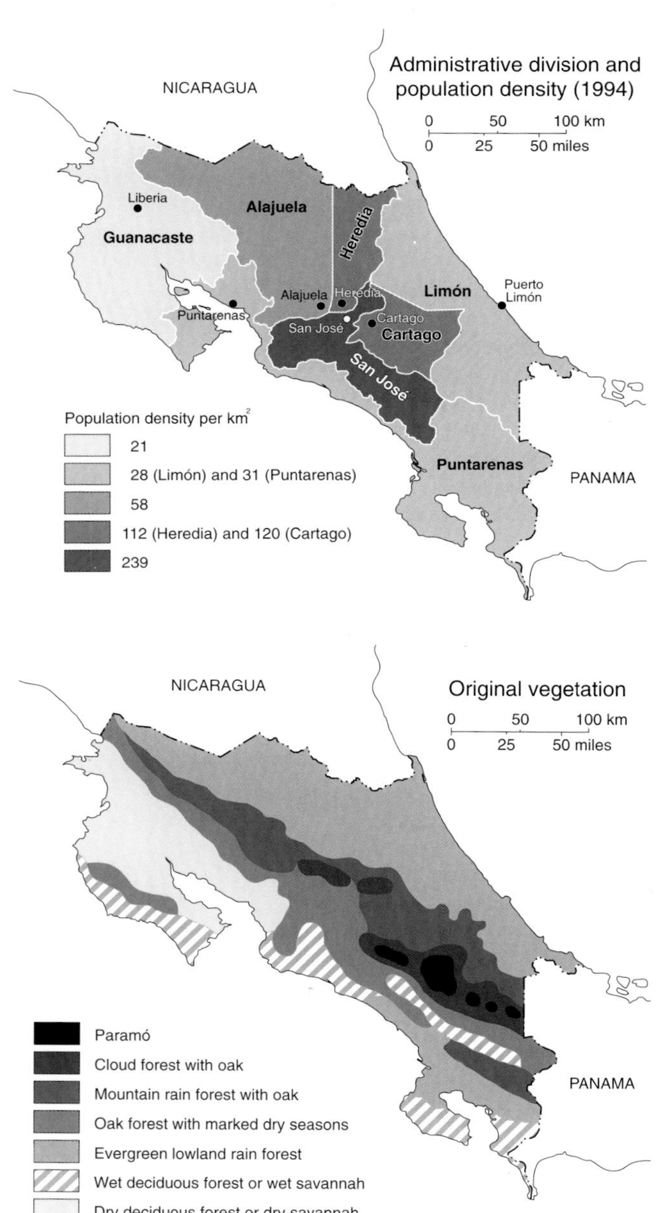

HISTORY AND POLITICS

Key historical dates: * eighth century: the Chorotegas, one of the most important of the Indian tribes, settle in Nicoya and Guanacaste * 1502: Columbus lands on the shore of Limón * 1563: first definitive Spanish settlement: Cartago * 17th-18th century: Costa Rica part of Guatemalan Captaincy-General, subject to the Vice-Kingdom of New Spain (Mexico) * 1821: independence; occupation by Mexico; population of Costa Rica 75,000 * 1823-1838: member of the United Provinces of Central America (confederation) * 1824: Juan Mora Fernández the first president; coffee growers are given free land; beginning of coffee exports * 1838: Costa Rica leaves confederation, ten years later the last links are severed * 1856: William Walker makes an unsuccessful attempt to subjugate Costa Rica * 1869: right to free education established in constitution * 1882: abolition of death penalty * 1889: elections; first form of democracy, although women, blacks, and Indians are not given the vote until 1949 * c. 1900: start of banana growing along the Caribbean coast * 1940-4: President Calderón carries out social reforms * 1948: elections give rise to civil war * 1948-9: junta of

José Figueres Ferrer; new constitution in which army is abolished * 1949: junta cedes power to elected president, Otillo Ulate Blanco * 1949 to 1970s: development of system of social provision * 1970s-1980s: debt crisis and retrenchment * 1980s: Costa Rica succeeds with difficulty in remaining outside the Nicaraguan civil war; Nicaraguan refugees * 1986-1990: Oscar Arias Sánchez president * 1987: Arias awarded Nobel Peace Prize * 1990s: rapidly increasing importance of tourism and export industries.
Constitution/administration: since 1949 presidential republic; unicameral parliament: *Congreso Constitucional,* 57 members; direct election of President and Congress every four years.
Head of State: Miguel Angel Rodriguez, since May 1998, in office until 2002.
Political parties: (number of seats in Congress since February 1998): Partido de Liberacíon Nacional (PLN, social-democrats, 23), Partido Unidad Social Cristiano (PUSC, Christian democrats, 27), and minority parties (Fuerza Democrática and Independents, 7).
Army: abolished December 1948; paramilitary police force (Guardia Civil and Guardia Rural): 7,200 troops.
Military expenditure as percentage of spending on health and education (1995): 2%.
*Membership of international organizations***:** United Nations and UN organizations, Organization of American States (OAS), the Latin-American Economic System (SELA), the Central American Common Market (MCCA), Inter-American Development Bank (IDB), Organization of Central American States (ODECA).
Media and communication: 451,000 main telephone lines in use and 46,500 mobile cellular telephones (1996); 980,000 radios (1997), and 525,000 TVs (1997). There are 50 AM, 43 FM, and 19 shortwave radio stations (1997); 6 TV stations and 11 repeaters (1997); and 2 Internet service providers (1999).

ECONOMY

Gross domestic product (GDP) (1999): $26 billion.
GDP per capita (1999): $7,100.
Unit of currency: colón (C); 1 colón = 100 céntimos; exhange rate per US$1: 300 (2000).
Inflation: 1999: 10.8%; 1996: 13.8%; 1995: 22.7%; 1994: 19.9%; 1980-1993: 22.1%; 1970-1980: 15.3%.
GDP growth: 2000: 1.4%; 1999: 7%; 1997 (est.): 2.2%; 1996: -0.8%; 1995: 2.5%; 1994: 4.5%; 1993: 6.1%; 1992: 7.7%; 1991: 2.3%; 1980-1993: 3.6%; 1970-1980: 5.7% per annum.
GDP by sector (1998): agriculture 14%, industry 22%, services 64%.
Fiscal deficit as % of GDP: 5% (1996); 3.5% (1995); 8.4% (1994).
Foreign debt (1998): $3.9 billion.
Foreign debt servicing as % of exports (1997): 12.5%.
Development aid per inhabitant (1993): $30.1.
Working population (1993): 1.14 million: agriculture 22.6%, mining 0.1%, construction 6.1%, industry 17.9%, trade 17.7%, transport and communication 4.7%, financial services 4.2%, government 25.1%, other 1.2%.
Unemployment (1998): 5.6% (underemployment 7.5%).
Exports: value 1999: $6.4 billion (1996: $2.86 billion, 1995: $2.6 billion); main exports (1992): manufactures 48% (including clothing, medicines, rubber products, glass, furniture; 6% produced in export zones), bananas 27%, coffee 11%, plants and flowers 4%,